Understanding the Old Testament

a narrative summary

by
David Nichols

2008
BookSurge Publishing

Understanding the Old Testament: A Narrative Summary

BookSurge Publishing
Charleston, South Carolina

Cover design by Heidi Goodhart
Printed in the United States of America

Visit www.booksurge.com to order additional copies.

CONTENTS

Acknowledgments

This project is the outgrowth of a Together in Ministry group funded by a grant from the Minister's Council of the American Baptist Churches/USA in conjunction with the Lilly Endowment Sustaining Pastoral Excellence program. Under the insightful leadership of Rev. Dan Buttry, ABC/USA Global Consultant for Peace and Justice, several of us have met over the past four years to read and discuss a number of books. Much of what we read dealt with what it means to be a missional church. It was through this group that I was introduced to N. T. Wright, Brian McLaren, Rob Bell and a host of other writers who have had a profound impact on my thinking. Those who have been with me in this discussion group from the beginning are:

- Rev. Wes Babian, First Baptist Church, Birmingham, MI

- Rev. William Walker, First Baptist Church of Detroit, Southfield, MI

- Rev. Jane Moschenrose, Wellspring Community Church, Farmington Hills, MI

Three others participated in the Together in Ministry group until their duties called them elsewhere: Rev. James Bolin, Rev. Michael Bryan, and Rev. Wungreiso Valui.

This project also owes much to the First Baptist Church of Royal Oak, Michigan, where I have served as pastor since 2004. I am particularly grateful to those who have met for Bible study every Tuesday morning for several years. The members of this group have patiently allowed me to experiment with various approaches to studying the Bible: Ruth Bertapelle, Nancy Cancel, Doris Diaz, Jo Gibson, Esther Giercek, Betty Gulish, Grace Harrison, Barbara Meyer, Earl "Bud" Page, Norma Page, Nobu Shimokochi, Joanne Smith, Jean Storer, and Ruth Walden.

Others from the church gave solid feedback as the manuscript was developing: Ben Barber IV, Diana Barber, Bruce Beaumont, Dave Brown, Lisa Carruthers, Young Key Chung, Dick Edgar, Sandra Grimm, Jim Higginbottom, Nan Hubbard, Rick Jones,

Nancy LaBeau, Amy Lyon, Dennis Schultz, Jeff Sparling, Ted Wedepohl, and Cindy Wodnicki.

In order to complete a first draft of this manuscript, I knew I would need to find a time and place to focus my efforts. The church gave me a month of vacation and study leave, and my sister, Judy Day, and her husband, Dick, graciously provided space for me in their Neosho, Missouri home.

After finishing the rough draft of a first manuscript, I wanted to get feedback from those whose opinions I value. I was delighted when nearly 100 agreed to do so!

Many pastors, seminary professors, or other professional church leaders provided helpful feedback: Rev. Allan Bendert, Rev. Ron Burks, Rev. Ron Cary, Rev. Charles Epperly, Rev. Jon Good, Dr. Maynard Hatch, Rev. Patricia Hernandez, Rev. Brian Johnson, Rev. Jane Moschenrose, Rev. K. S. Murphy, Bridget Nemzek, Rev. Jim Pool, Dr. Ken Potts, Tim Renaud, Dr. Douglas Sharp, Rev. Ed Sladek, Rev. David Swink, and Dr. Michael Williams.

Several family and friends became involved in the project: Virginia Beehn, Pat Curtis, Diane Hummel, Vince Lindstrom, Sue Miller, Jacqueline Myers, Patty Nichols, Ron Paden, Kay Pavell, Jackie Pyle, Betsy Sabel, Bev Thornton, and Doug Vos.

One member of my church, Susan Beaumont, is a consultant with Alban Institute. The excellent feedback she gave me in the early part of the writing process helped immensely.

Another person who proved most helpful was Veda Boyd Jones, a friend of nearly fifty years, who has published more books than I could ever hope to do.

Heidi Goodhart, a multi-talented artist, editor and marketing consultant, designed the cover and assisted me at every step of the editing process.

Dayna Fick has helped with final preparation of the manuscript and with development of a website that includes a discussion board and blog. Check it out at: www.utotbook.com

Special mention must go to my father-in-law, Dr. Charles Berg, partly because he would expect nothing less! As the first to read my early chapters, his critique and encouragement were great.

My wife, Linnea Berg, has given me invaluable encouragement and feedback. In twenty years of reviewing my sermons she has demonstrated an uncanny ability to let me know when I'm on target and when I'm missing the mark. She also has given me the freedom to spend countless hours at the computer.

Thanks to all – and especially to God for giving people of faith an ancient story that never grows old.

December 2008

PREFACE:
THE BIBLE IS A STORY

The Bible has been called "the world's least-read best-seller." In a lifetime of studying and teaching the Bible, I've heard countless people say they wish they knew what the Bible said. Some say they were never taught the Bible. Others say they've read the Bible for years, but still feel clueless about much of it.

The fact that the Bible is difficult to understand should not surprise us. After all, it consists of 66 separate books chronicling a period of over 2,000 years and reflecting the impact of Sumerian, Egyptian, Babylonian, Persian, Greek, Roman and other cultures. It is considerably longer than virtually any other book people might consider reading, and it was originally written in Hebrew and Greek, with Aramaic showing up in a few places. No wonder people find the Bible hard to understand no matter what method they use to read it.

- *Some read the Bible sequentially*, determined to make it from beginning to end with a "through-the-Bible-in-a-year" guide. By the end of January, such readers will have read Genesis and the first part of Exodus only to encounter instructions for building a Tabernacle. Next comes Leviticus with details on burnt sacrifices and lengthy descriptions of what is to be considered clean and unclean. Only the most faithful are able to make it through February.

- *Some read the Bible thematically*, aided by a Bible study guide. There are many such books that follow a common format: every topic has a number of sentences, each with one or more missing words to be filled in by looking up a verse of the Bible. Those who write such studies make sure that students learn from the Bible exactly what they are supposed to learn. Little attention is paid to the context of the verse and the student is rarely encouraged to struggle with the text or reflect on what it might mean.

- ***Some read the Bible mysteriously***, hoping to tease out hidden meanings from some rather obscure passages in the writings of the prophets. The past two centuries reveal multiple examples of people who thought they could determine exactly how and when the world would end. Although none of these speculations has come to pass, there are still plenty of people who keep trying to explain what comes next.

- ***Some read the Bible aggressively***, looking for any ammunition they can find to use against those who disagree with them. The problem with this approach is that the Bible can be used to prove all kinds of things. The notorious atheist, Madelyn Murray O'Hair, told a group of students at Harvard, "Don't quote the Bible thinking it proves your point because you can make the Bible say anything you want." She went on to give some outrageous examples of what the Bible "proves." The portions of Scripture she used were taken out of context, of course, but no more so than preachers throughout history have done to justify slavery, male superiority, capital punishment, war, racial prejudice, and a host of other things. Interestingly, Ms. O'Hair was so rude, crude and frequently obscene in her remarks that one Harvard student was overheard saying, "She sure makes it hard to be an atheist!"

- ***Some read the Bible devotionally***, looking for verses that are comforting or inspirational. This often works well, but ignoring context can sometimes yield strange results. Consider the example of the man who opened the Bible randomly to find his 'verse of the day,' and came to Matthew 27:5: "Judas went out and hanged himself." Deciding that wouldn't do, he opened his Bible again, this time to Luke 10:37: "Go, and do likewise." Figuring that the third time would be the charm, he opened it once more and found John 13:27: "What you are about to do, do quickly."

The problem with all of these approaches is that they inevitably miss the big picture by not understanding that *the Bible is a story*. It isn't a massive collection of propositional truths to be studied, memorized, and brought out as needed. Neither is it a compilation of secret writings that, if properly deciphered, reveal the deep mysteries of God. *The Bible tells the story of God acting in the world to restore creation to its original purpose after people had made a real mess of things.* Reading the story helps us understand who God is, who we are, and what our relationship with God and each other is supposed to be.

This book tells the first part of that long story in summarized form in order to grasp the big picture of the Old Testament. A sequel to this book will do the same for the New Testament.

The chapters that follow describe how God called Abraham and promised that his descendants would be a blessing for the entire world. Following centuries in Egypt as slaves and decades of wandering in the wilderness, the "children of Abraham" entered the Promised Land. For the next 200 years they were a disorganized collection of twelve tribes occasionally brought together by a ruler who rallied them to defeat their enemies. The tribes were united as a nation for less than 100 years under David and Solomon. Civil war followed with the northern kingdom, Israel, lasting 200 years before being conquered and dispersed by the Assyrians. The people of the southern kingdom, Judah, were taken into captivity by the Babylonians 130 years after that. Following more than 50 years in exile, the next generation of Jews was sent back to rebuild Jerusalem and the Temple – tasks that took another century to complete.

This is the point at which the Old Testament ends, but it is by no means the end of the story. Many who read the Old Testament and then the New Testament come away with the impression that they are reading two different stories – one about a God of wrath, and the other about a God of love. Such perceptions are partly due to people being unaware of what took place during the 400 years that separate the Old and New Testaments. The epilogue in this book covers that period of history in a way that shows the connection between the two. Without that essential information, much of what we see in the New Testament makes little sense.

It is a bit like watching a movie: miss the first half and you'll struggle to understand the rest. The Old Testament provides the context for what Jesus says and does. Understanding the Old Testament may not be easy, but it is important.

This book is a narrative summary written from the perspective of the Old Testament era and the centuries that followed until the birth of Jesus. Passages later understood to be about Jesus are not interpreted as such here. For instance, Psalm 22 and Isaiah 53 powerfully capture the suffering of Jesus, but no one before Jesus understood these passages to speak of a Messiah.

I am tempted to say this book is *only* a summary of the Bible with no interpretation added, but such a claim would be naïve. Every time we quote the Bible our subjectivity comes through, if only by the choice of which passages we choose to quote and which we choose to ignore. My understanding of what the Bible says has given shape to and been shaped by my spiritual journey.

My childhood was spent in a conservative American Baptist church where I memorized many Bible verses, but understood few. During high school, I drifted from whatever faith I might have had earlier, but came back to faith at Harvard University through the ministry of Campus Crusade for Christ and Inter-Varsity Christian Fellowship. After college, I went to Northern Baptist Theological Seminary where I fought hard to defend an evangelical faith that I barely understood against what I thought were the godless attacks of critical authors we were required to read. Even though years of teaching and preaching have allowed me to study the Bible intensively, I feel that I'm only beginning to grasp much of the Bible's message. I've had a lot to learn, and a lot to unlearn. I still do.

I have sought to stay close to the biblical text in this book, and have done little to show the relevance of what the Old Testament says to contemporary life. Such a task is beyond the scope of this book and is the responsibility of each reader. Questions at the end of each chapter, however, are provided to assist readers in connecting the story of the Bible to the story of our world today. Readers may find it particularly rewarding to find others who would read this book and discuss the questions. A boxed number refers to a related question at the end of the chapter.

With the exception of a few transitional sentences added here and there for continuity, everything in the chapters that follow is based on the Bible. I had originally thought to footnote each sentence to show its source, but decided this would be too cumbersome for the reader. Therefore each paragraph is footnoted to show the passages from which it originates.

Although the nature of this book does not lend itself to citing other writings, I have certainly been influenced by the various authors of the *New Interpreters' Bible*.[1] I am also particularly indebted to N. T. Wright for *The New Testament and the People of God*,[2] which has given me an appreciation of how Jews in the first century would have understood the Hebrew Scriptures.

In terms of the miraculous events described throughout the Old Testament narrative, it is my hope that skeptical readers will withhold judgment on whether such things are possible, and simply let the story unfold. Avoiding disputes about the six days of creation, Jonah being swallowed by a whale or Elisha's floating axe might make it easier for you to grasp the story of the Bible as a whole. It may even allow the story of the Bible to grasp you – a possibility that could alter your perspective on the nature of miracles.

My intention in writing this book is that those who read it will be more likely to read the Bible – and more likely to understand

---

[1] New Interpreter's Bible; Leander A. Keck, editor (Nashville, TN: Abingdon Press, 1994)

[2] The New Testament and the People of God: Christian Origins and the Question of God; N. T. Wright (Minneapolis, MN: Augsburg Fortress Publishers, 1992)

what they read. My prayer is that this will happen in the pages that follow.

Please feel free to contact me with questions or comments you have regarding *Understanding the Old Testament: A Narrative Summary.* My website is:

www.utotbook.com

CHAPTER 1:
IN THE BEGINNING

All was darkness and chaos until God said, "Let there be light," and the world as we know it came to be. God continued the process of creation day by day until the land, sea and sky had taken shape, and there were plants and creatures living in them. On the sixth day, Adam ("the man" in Hebrew) and Eve ("mother of all" in Hebrew) were created in God's own image, and in intimate partnership with each other. On the seventh day, God rested.[1]

God looked at everything that was being created and saw how good it was. Adam and Eve had an abundant supply of food in the Garden of Eden, and the freedom to do almost anything they wanted. The only thing they were *required* to do was to take care of the world God had given them. The only thing they were *forbidden* to do was to eat fruit from the tree of the knowledge of good and evil.[2]

Unfortunately, Adam and Eve found themselves unable to resist either the lure of the forbidden fruit or the lies of the snake that told them this fruit would make them like God.[3]

Adam and Eve soon discovered the error of their ways. Eating the forbidden fruit indeed gave them knowledge of good and evil, but at a horrible price:

- It cost them their *innocence*, as they hastily covered themselves out of shame at their nakedness;

- It cost them their *joy*, as they cowered in fear when they heard God approaching;

- It cost them their *integrity*, as they blamed others for the foolish choices each had made;

---

[1] Genesis 1:1-25; 2:1-7; 2:22
[2] Genesis 1:28-31; 2:15-17
[3] Genesis 1:27; 3:1-4

- It cost them their *hope,* as they were expelled from the Garden into a wilderness of weeds and thorns; and,

- It cost them their *immortality,* as they were now denied access to Eden's tree of life.[4]

Though Adam and Eve suffered the consequences of their actions, God did not simply abandon them. God's compassion was shown by making leather clothes to protect them from the harsh environment in which they were now to spend their lives.[5]

3 Adam and Eve lived as best they could in the wilderness, starting a family and rejoicing at the birth of their sons, Cain and Abel. As time passed, however, problems arose. Abel offered one of his animals as a sacrifice to God, and Cain offered some of the crops he had grown. Abel's offering was accepted by God, but Cain's offering was not. Furious that God favored his brother, Cain lured Abel into a field and killed him. When God asked where Abel was, Cain replied, "Am I my brother's keeper?" God told Cain he had better listen because his brother's blood was crying out to God for justice.[6]

God told Cain he would suffer the consequences of his actions by leaving his family and going deeper into the wilderness. God did not abandon Cain completely, but showed compassion by placing a mark on him that would be a deterrent to any who might seek to kill him in his travels.[7]

This was not a promising beginning for humanity, and the generations that followed fared no better. God saw the extent to which evil and wickedness were flourishing, and was deeply grieved by it. Eventually, evil became so pervasive that God decided to start over – not by creating a new world, but by working through Noah, a good man who was willing to do

---

[4] Genesis 3:7-23

[5] Genesis 3:21

[6] Genesis 4:1-10

[7] Genesis 4:11-16

everything God asked of him.[8]

God told Noah to build a huge ark in which his family and many animals would be rescued from a cataclysmic flood. Although what he was asked to do must have sounded ridiculous, Noah did everything as instructed. Forty days of torrential rains followed, turning Noah's world into an ocean. When the floodwaters receded, Noah came safely out of the ark with his family and the animals. Everything was ready for a fresh start, and God said the rainbow would be a perpetual sign that never again would such destruction come upon the earth.[9]

God pronounced blessings on Noah and his family, telling them to multiply throughout the earth and setting forth simple conditions under which they were to live:

1. Don't eat the blood of any animal; and,

2. Don't shed the blood of any person.

Consuming animal blood and spilling human blood would be considered an offense against God who gives life to all.[10]

The fresh start God gave Noah and his descendants soon went awry. Noah planted a vineyard and celebrated the wine he made by drinking so much that he passed out naked in his tent. One of his sons, Ham, entered the tent, saw Noah's condition, and joked to his brothers about it. The brothers, Shem and Japheth, discreetly covered their father's nakedness. When Noah discovered what had happened, his anger at his shameless son boiled over into curses upon Ham and his descendants.[11]

As the generations came and went, the world that followed Noah looked no better than the one that had preceded him. In spite of God's warnings about the shedding of blood, mighty warriors like Nimrod were praised and honored. Others wanted

---

[8] Genesis 6:5-12

[9] Genesis 6:13-22; 7:1-24; 8:1-22; 9:1-17

[10] Genesis 9:4-7

[11] Genesis 9:20-25

to make a name for themselves by building a tower in Babel tall enough to reach the heavens. God put an end to that project by giving the people different languages. Unable to make sense of each other's babbling, they separated into groups by language and moved into different areas of the world.[12]

Noah's descendants multiplied throughout the earth as God had instructed, but in ways that led to misunderstanding and conflict. God decided something new would have to be done if humanity was ever to discover the goodness of life intended by God from the beginning.

---

[12] Genesis 10:8-32; 11:1-9

Questions for Reflection/Discussion

1. As the world began, God addressed the darkness and chaos by speaking words that brought transforming light and order. Where in today's world do we find darkness and chaos still in need of transformation?

2. Adam and Eve paid a terrible price for giving in to the lure of forbidden fruit and the lies of a deceiving creature. What temptations and deceptions are people susceptible to in today's world? Why do people so easily make bad choices?

3. After the senseless murder of his brother, Cain was told to listen because Abel's blood was calling out to God. Where does the blood of innocent victims of war and violence call out to God for justice today? Are we listening?

4. One of Noah's sons found his father's situation entertaining; the other two sons did what they could to restore their father's dignity and respect. What can we do to restore the dignity and respect of those who are the butt of cruel jokes and taunts today?

5. Evil spread like wildfire in the generations that preceded Noah and in the ones that followed him. Are there more recent times in which evil has become pervasive? What are some examples?

CHAPTER 2:
ABRAHAM, ISAAC AND JACOB

God's plan to give humanity a fresh start through Noah had not put an end to the world's problems. God now chose a man whose story of life and faith would be a source of blessing for all people. The one chosen for this honor, however, was more than a little surprised to be God's choice. Abram, who had no children after many years of marriage, was told by God that he would have countless descendants, and that this would happen in a new home hundreds of miles away.[1]

In spite of the strangeness and seeming impossibility of what God had promised, Abram gathered up everything he had and began the long and difficult journey. Entering Canaan from the north, he traveled south by stages until he came to the dry and barren land that he discovered was to be the site of his new life.[2]

[1] Sometimes Abram's faith faltered. When famine became severe in his new land, he sought refuge in Egypt. Perhaps because he was worried that God did not seem to be taking care of him, Abram sought to guarantee his own safety by asking his wife, Sarai, to say that she was his sister. Abram's plan went from bad to worse until God intervened to set things right.[3]

At other times, Abram was willing to place his life in God's hands. When his nephew, Lot, complained that Abram's servants were taking the best land to graze their flocks, Abram told Lot to choose whatever lands he wanted and Abram would take the rest. Lot chose the richer lands near Sodom and Abram made no complaint when he ended up with the less desirable hill country.[4]

Lot may have ended up with the better land, but he also ended up with bigger problems. Several kings joined forces to attack the

---

[1] Genesis 11:30; 12:1-4; 13:14-17

[2] Genesis 12:4-9

[3] Genesis 12:10-20

[4] Genesis 13:8-11

wealthy region around Sodom. After winning the battle, the kings took everything of value – including Lot's family and others from the city who could serve as slaves.[5]

After hearing what had happened, Abram raised an army and set off in pursuit. He was able to rescue the people who had been captured and recover all the plunder that had been taken as well. On the way home, Melchizedek, the king of Salem, treated Abram and the others with great hospitality. Abram gave Melchizedek a tenth of all his plunder because of the blessing he had received. Abram gave the remainder of the plunder to the king of Sodom, refusing to accept any portion lest he be accused of enriching himself at the expense of others.[6]

In spite of such decisions, Abram's wealth continued to increase until he had hundreds of servants and thousands of animals. Abram still felt impoverished, however, because he had no children. God came to him again and reaffirmed that Abram's descendants would one day be as numerous as stars in the sky.[7]

Abram's wife came up with her own plan to make this happen. After ten years had passed without God's promise of a child being fulfilled, Sarai told Abram to sleep with her Egyptian servant, Hagar, so that he would at least have some chance of having an heir.[8]

Not surprisingly, this plan did not go smoothly. As soon as Hagar knew she was pregnant, she began to look at Sarai with contempt. Sarai complained to Abram, who told her she was free to deal with her servant however she wanted. The abuse that followed brought Hagar to a point of desperation. She sought to hide in the desert, but an angel found her and let her know that God was aware of her plight. The angel promised that the child born to Hagar would have many descendants, but also many

---

[5] Genesis 14:1-12

[6] Genesis 14:13-24

[7] Genesis 13:1-2; 15:1-6

[8] Genesis 16:1-4

enemies. Though such words were not exactly reassuring, Hagar took courage from knowing that God was aware of her situation. Hagar went back to Sarai and gave birth to Ishmael.[9]

More years passed and the time came for God to fulfill his promise to Abram and Sarai. The first thing God did was to give them new names: Abraham, "father of many nations," and Sarah, "woman of high esteem." Sarah's name was ironic, given the low esteem with which her own servant held her.[10]

3 God told Abraham and Sarah they would have a son the next year. Given that they had been waiting more than twenty years for this to happen, and that Abraham was now almost 100 and Sarah only ten years younger, the whole thing sounded absurd. God assured them it was no joke. God also told them from now on all their boys and men would need to be circumcised as a reminder of God's promise being fulfilled.[11]

Though the birth of Isaac, the child promised to Abraham and Sarah, was met with great rejoicing, Sarah's resentment toward Hagar soon reappeared. Determined that Ishmael should receive no inheritance, Sarah convinced Abraham to banish Hagar and Ishmael to the wilderness where they would surely die. God rescued them however, and promised Hagar that Ishmael would survive the wilderness to give rise to a mighty desert people.[12]

Some time later, God told Abraham that Sodom, the city where Lot lived, would be destroyed. Sodom had a terrible reputation because its people were arrogant, overfed and unconcerned about helping the poor and needy. Because he was upset that the righteous would be destroyed with the wicked, Abraham asked God to spare the city if even a small number of good people could be found. God agreed, and sent visitors to Sodom to see how the people treated them. The results were shocking: Lot invited the travelers into his home as guests, but the rest of the

---

[9] Genesis 16:6-16

[10] Genesis 17:1-15

[11] Genesis 17:16-27; 18:12

[12] Genesis 21:1-21

city viewed the visitors as nothing more than helpless foreigners to be raped and abused. Before destruction came upon the city, God created a means of escape for Lot and his family. Lot's wife went with him, but kept looking back and longing for what she had left behind. At the moment of Sodom's destruction, she became a pillar of salt.[13]

Over the years, Abraham learned much about what it meant to trust God, but the day came when his faith was put to its greatest test. God told Abraham to take his son and offer him as a human sacrifice. On the journey to Mt. Moriah, Isaac asked what was to be sacrificed. Abraham responded, "God himself will provide a lamb." At the moment Abraham was about to take his son's life, God opened Abraham's eyes to see a ram caught in a nearby thicket. Abraham sacrificed the ram in gratitude to God for sparing his son.[14]

4

When Isaac was old enough to be married, Abraham decided his son should marry someone from his homeland rather than a local, Canaanite girl. Abraham sent one of his servants on the long journey to find a suitable wife. The servant met Rebekah, a beautiful young woman who revealed her character by not only sharing her water with him, but drawing enough to satisfy all his thirsty camels. Such a woman was an answer to his prayers.[15]

Rebekah returned with Abraham's servant and became Isaac's wife. After twenty years of being childless, she gave birth to fraternal twins who had little in common. The older brother, Esau, grew up to be an adventurer and hunter. The younger brother, Jacob, preferred to stay close to home. Both parents had their favorites: Isaac loved Esau and Rebekah loved Jacob. The situation was ripe for conflict.[16]

5

The first sign of trouble came when Esau was on his way home from a long, unsuccessful hunt. He was famished when he came

[13] Genesis 18:16-33; 19:1-17; Ezekiel 16:49

[14] Genesis 22:1-18

[15] Genesis 24:1-20

[16] Genesis 25:21-28

upon Jacob cooking some stew. Rather than simply sharing with his brother, Jacob insisted on being given Esau's birthright in return. Esau gave Jacob what he wanted. After all, what good was his right to receive a double portion of his father's estate if he died of starvation first?[17]

The conflict between Jacob and Esau escalated as Isaac's eyesight faded and the end of his life drew near. Wanting to give a special blessing to his favorite son, Isaac asked Esau to kill some wild game and prepare a special meal for him. Rebekah overheard what Isaac said and saw an opportunity to gain further advantage for Jacob. She fixed the meal for Isaac and asked Jacob to take it to him, pretending to be Esau all the while. Rebekah even put lamb's wool on Jacob's hands and arms to give the impression that he was hairy like Esau. Rebekah's scheme worked, and Isaac pronounced a powerful blessing on Jacob. When Esau discovered that he had been cheated once again, he was furious.[18]

Esau was determined to take Jacob's life as soon as Isaac was gone. Rebekah learned of Esau's intention and figured out a way to rescue Jacob. She convinced Isaac that Jacob should not marry a Canaanite girl, but should return to their homeland for a wife.[19]

Although Jacob had acted deceitfully time and again, Isaac sent him on his journey with yet another blessing. On the journey, God appeared to Jacob in a dream that showed a ladder reaching up to heaven. God confirmed in the dream that the covenant with Abraham would be fulfilled through Jacob, who would have more descendants than he could imagine and a land that would always be their home. In fact, the whole world would be blessed through him.[20]

When Jacob arrived in his homeland, he lived with his uncle Laban, and fell in love with Rachel, Laban's daughter. Jacob

---

[17] Genesis 25:29-34

[18] Genesis 27:1-36

[19] Genesis 27:42-46; 28:1-2

[20] Genesis 28:3-15

agreed to work seven years for the right to marry Rachel, but when the marriage finally took place, Laban sent his older daughter, Leah, into the marriage tent instead. Jacob discovered the next morning what had happened and confronted his uncle about the deception. Laban explained that it was the custom that the oldest daughter must always be married before the younger. If Jacob still wanted Rachel, however, he could marry her as well if he was willing to work another seven years.[21]

Thus Jacob the Deceiver became Jacob the Deceived. He now had two wives, but loved only one. God saw that the real victim in this story was not Jacob, but Leah, the unloved wife. God richly blessed Leah by giving her four sons. This did not sit well with Rachel, the wife who had Jacob's heart but none of his children. Hoping to be at least a surrogate mother, Rachel gave her servant, Bilhah, to be a wife for Jacob, and when two sons were born to her servant, Rachel felt like she was gaining on her sister. Determined to regain the advantage, Leah gave her own servant, Zilpah, to Jacob, with two more sons as the result. Leah then bribed Rachel into letting Jacob start sleeping with her again and two more sons and a daughter were born. Refusing to give up hope, Rachel eventually became pregnant and gave birth to Joseph.[22]

Jacob's family and fortune had grown and he was now ready to return to Canaan a wealthy man. Knowing that his prosperity had made Laban and his sons jealous and angry, Jacob decided it would be best to slip away in the middle of the night. When Laban found out what had happened, he went after Jacob. It looked like things could get nasty until God appeared to Laban and warned him to be careful how he treated his son-in-law. The expected confrontation was resolved peacefully, with Jacob agreeing not to mistreat Laban's daughters and Laban agreeing not to attack Jacob.[23]

---

[21] Genesis 29:13-27

[22] Genesis 29:31-35; 30:1-24

[23] Genesis 30:25-26; 31:1-53

With that confrontation behind him, Jacob now worried about facing Esau. He sent messengers to let his brother know he was back in the country, and Esau sent a small army to greet him. Expecting the worst, Jacob prayed that God would deliver him from his brother's wrath. The only way Jacob could think of to pacify his brother was to overwhelm him with gifts.[24]

6 As Jacob waited for Esau's arrival, he wrestled all night with a stranger. Though Jacob was unable to prevail, he persisted to the point where God gave him both a blessing and a permanent limp reminding him always of this night. Jacob was also given a new name: Israel, the one who struggles with God.[25]

Despite Jacob's worst fears, when Esau finally arrived, he ran to meet Jacob, hugged and kissed him, and wept tears of joy to see him again. Esau didn't want Jacob's lavish gifts, but Jacob insisted he accept them. Jacob refused Esau's offers of help, and moved to a different part of the country to build a new life.[26]

Some time later, God spoke to Jacob again and told him to leave his new home and move to Bethel. In order for Jacob and his family's new life to be what God intended, they would have to get rid of all their foreign religious objects and commit to worshipping and serving the one true God.[27]

God appeared to Jacob yet again, confirming that all of God's promises to Abraham would be fulfilled through Jacob's sons and their descendants. Rachel died giving birth to Benjamin, the twelfth son of Jacob.[28]

Just as Jacob had loved Rachel more than his other wives, it was obvious that Joseph, her firstborn, was Jacob's favorite son. This did not sit well with his older brothers, especially when Joseph made it a point to tell Jacob whenever his brothers did something

---

[24] Genesis 32:3-21

[25] Genesis 32:22-30

[26] Genesis 33:1-17

[27] Genesis 35:2-4

[28] Genesis 35:9-18

wrong. Jacob made things worse by giving Joseph a multi-colored cloak, the clothing of a prince.[29]

What was already a bad situation grew worse when Joseph told his brothers about two dreams, both of which featured people bowing down to him. It wasn't long before his brothers' jealousy and hatred boiled over into a plot to kill him. The opportunity came when Joseph was sent to check up on his brothers as they were watching their father's sheep in the wilderness. They decided to kill Joseph and throw his body down an empty well. Reuben, Jacob's oldest son, said it would be better to throw Joseph down the well alive. He said this, hoping for a chance to come back later and rescue his brother.[30]

Before Reuben could carry out his plan, the situation took an unexpected turn. A caravan of slave-traders passed by and the brothers decided it would be better to sell Joseph into slavery than to be responsible for his death. To convince their father that Joseph had died, they soaked his fancy cloak in lamb's blood and took it home.[31]

Joseph was taken to Egypt and sold to Potiphar, the captain of Pharaoh's palace guard, who quickly saw that this new servant was a man of great ability. The captain put Joseph in charge of his entire household. Everything went well until Potiphar's wife noticed how handsome Joseph was. He resisted her advances, but she persisted until she was able to lure Joseph into her bedroom. When he still refused to have sex with her, she accused him of rape. Potiphar put him in prison, but Joseph's situation turned out better than expected. The warden quickly recognized Joseph's abilities and put him in charge of all the prisoners.[32]

Time passed and two of Pharaoh's personal servants were thrown in prison and had dreams there that disturbed them. Joseph interpreted their dreams, saying that in three days, one

---

[29] Genesis 37:2-4

[30] Genesis 37:5-22

[31] Genesis 37:25-35

[32] Genesis 37:36; 39:2-23

servant would be reinstated and the other beheaded. Things happened just as Joseph had predicted, but the servant who was reinstated did nothing about the debt of gratitude he owed.[33]

Two years passed and Pharaoh had dreams that troubled him greatly because none of his advisers had any idea what they meant. It was then that Pharaoh's servant remembered Joseph's remarkable ability to interpret dreams. Joseph was brought to the palace and told Pharaoh that both of his dreams had the same meaning: seven years of bumper crops would be followed by seven years of severe famine. Joseph advised Pharaoh to find a good manager who could build sufficient reserves during the years of abundance to see them through the famine. Pharaoh thought it was a good plan and concluded that there was no one better than Joseph to make it happen. Joseph was put in a position of incredible power, second only to Pharaoh himself. He was given an Egyptian wife who eventually bore him two sons: Manasseh and Ephraim.[34]

Joseph's plan worked well; when the famine worsened, people came from near and far to buy grain from Pharaoh's storehouses. Eventually, Jacob's brothers found it necessary to come to Egypt as well, having heard that this was the only place where grain could still be bought. Joseph's brothers bowed down before him just as his dream had foretold, but they didn't recognize him. After all, Joseph now looked like an Egyptian, and who could have imagined that someone sold into slavery would end up in such a position?[35]

To gain some small revenge, Joseph accused his brothers of coming to Egypt as enemy spies. They denied the charges, but Joseph said he would not believe them unless they returned with the younger brother they claimed to have left behind. Joseph told them one of the brothers would be imprisoned until the others returned. The brothers were convinced they were being punished

---

[33] Genesis 40:1-23

[34] Genesis 41:1-45

[35] Genesis 37:5-8; 41:46-57; 42:1-8

by God for the evil way they had treated Joseph earlier.[36]

The brothers returned home with the grain they needed, but Jacob was distressed that Simeon had been left behind and his youngest son would have to go with them on their next trip. Though it felt to him like his family was being destroyed one son at a time, there was no relief to the draught and Jacob decided he would have to send all his sons to Egypt once again for grain.[37]

Everything went well until the brothers began their return trip to Canaan. Having hidden an item of great value in Benjamin's grain sack, Joseph sent his servants to arrest all the brothers. They protested their innocence and invited the servants to search everything. The other brothers were devastated when the missing object was found in the sack of Joseph's youngest brother. As Benjamin was being arrested, Judah offered to be Joseph's slave in his place.[38]

When his brothers returned under arrest, Joseph could carry on the ruse no longer. He was deeply moved that his **7** brothers had gone through such a dramatic change and had such obvious love for their youngest brother, the one who had replaced Joseph as their father's favorite. Joseph revealed his identity, weeping so loudly that the rest of Pharaoh's servants wondered what was wrong. Joseph told his brothers that he no longer held against them the evil things they had done to him.[39]

Joseph sent his brothers back to Canaan with instructions to let Jacob know what had happened and to bring his entire household to Egypt to be spared from the famine. Pharaoh approved of Joseph's plan and promised that his family would have the best land in all Egypt and many gifts besides.[40]

Although Jacob had trouble believing that Joseph was alive and

---

[36] Genesis 42:9-21
[37] Genesis 42:29-38; 43:1-14
[38] Genesis 44:1-35
[39] Genesis 45:1-8
[40] Genesis 45:9-20

ruling in Egypt, he moved there with his entire household. On the journey, God appeared to Jacob with two promises: I will be with you in Egypt and I will bring your descendants back to Canaan.[41]

Not wanting his family to be assimilated fully into Egypt, Joseph told his brothers to tell Pharaoh that they were shepherds. He knew this would motivate Pharaoh to have Joseph's family live apart from everyone else because Egyptians despised shepherds and would not want to live near any of them. Thus Joseph's family was given their own land in Goshen, some of the best land in the entire country.[42]

Pharaoh's property benefited greatly from Joseph's management. As the famine continued, Pharaoh became extremely wealthy. When people had no more money, they paid for grain by giving their livestock to Pharaoh. When they had no more livestock, people gave their land and their lives to Pharaoh. Through Joseph's business acumen, the whole country became indebted to Pharaoh.[43]

8 As the end of Jacob's life drew near, he brought his sons before him, pronouncing blessings or woes on each one from oldest to youngest:

- Woe to Reuben for having slept with his father's mistress;

- Woe to Simeon and Levi for their violent tempers and murderous ways;

- Blessings to Judah, who would prosper and rule rightly over his brothers;

- Blessings to Zebulun, who would live by the sea and be a haven for ships;

- Woe to Isaachar, who would submit to forced labor;

---

[41] Genesis 45:25-28; 46:1-4

[42] Genesis 46:31-34; 47:1-6

[43] Genesis 47:13-21

- Blessings to Dan, who would provide justice for his people;

- Woe to Gad, who would be attacked by raiders;

- Blessings to Asher, who would always have rich food;

- Blessings to Naphtali, who would enjoy freedom;

- Blessings to Joseph, who has overcome evil;

- Woe to Benjamin for his warring ways.[44]

Jacob pronounced a powerful blessing on both of Joseph's sons as well. Jacob's last request was that one day his bones be carried back to Canaan where he could be laid to rest with his ancestors, Abraham, Sarah, Isaac and Rebekah.[45]

Following Jacob's death, Joseph's brothers once again feared that he might take his revenge on them. They begged Joseph to forgive them, and Joseph reassured them he held no grudge. After all, out of their most evil intentions, God had accomplished something truly good.[46]

---

[44] Genesis 49:2-27
[45] Genesis 48:8-22; 49:19-32
[46] Genesis 50:15-21

Questions for Reflection/Discussion

1. Abram's lack of faith led him to lie to Pharaoh. This made life safer for Abram, but it made his wife vulnerable to unwanted advances or even sexual assault. Have your fears ever made life difficult for someone you loved? In what situations have you found it hardest to trust that everything would be okay?

2. Hagar was an Egyptian slave most likely given as a handmaiden to Sarai by Pharaoh when Sarai was part of his harem. Sarai then gave Hagar to Abram in order that he might father a child. A woman being passed from person to person against her will is abhorrent, but what are some examples of attitudes, customs or practices that treat women unfairly in our day?

3. God's promise of a son to Abraham and Sarah in their old age sounded absurd. Have you ever been told something about God that you found hard to believe? As you have grown older, have you found it harder or easier to believe in God?

4. It is hard not to recoil in horror when we read that God asked Abraham to offer his son as a human sacrifice. Abraham seems not to have shared our outrage at such a request, probably because human sacrifice was a common element in the religions of that day. The purpose of such sacrifices was to gain divine favor or avoid divine wrath. This story is about something else because it ends with God providing a lamb to be offered in place of Abraham's son, a definite foreshadowing of what would happen with Jesus far in the future. Do people still worry about gaining God's favor or avoiding God's wrath? In what situations might someone seek to bargain with God today?

5. Jacob and Esau were different and each was the favorite of a parent. What draws a parent to one child more than to another? What impact does such favoritism have on children? How should parents deal with this?

6. Jacob struggled with God, like a child wrestling with a parent. This shows both the courage and persistence of Jacob and the compassion and tenderness of God. Have there been times in your life when you needed to show courage and persistence? What are some examples? Are you more likely to think of God as being compassionate and tender or angry and demanding? What do you think has most shaped your image of God?

7. Over time, Jacob's sons underwent a dramatic change from being angry enough to kill Joseph to being willing to sacrifice their lives for Benjamin. Have you seen a profound change take place in someone's life? What do you think might have brought about such a change?

8. Jacob pronounced blessings and woes upon his sons before he died. We don't have a formal structure for doing anything quite like that today, but parents still have ways of giving or denying approval to their children. How did your parents communicate their approval or disapproval of your behavior? To what extent do you think this made a lasting impact on your life?

CHAPTER 3:
EXODUS FROM EGYPT

Four hundred years is a long time, and as the centuries passed, the Egyptians forgot the circumstances under which the Israelites had come to them. They made slaves of the Israelites, and then became concerned when their numbers grew. After all, it was nice to have more slaves who could work, but it was scary to have more slaves who could revolt. One Pharaoh decided something had to be done.[1]

His first plan was to put cruel and demanding slave masters over the Israelites. Although this caused them to suffer, they grew even more numerous during their years of harsh treatment.[2]

1 Pharaoh's next plan was crueler yet. He told the Israelite midwives to kill every male newborn, but to let the daughters live. Because the midwives found ways to avoid being part of such a slaughter, Pharaoh took his plan to the next step by issuing a public decree: every newborn Israelite boy was to be thrown into the Nile River.[3]

One baby was rescued from this fate, both by his mother's determination and by God's intervention. When baby Moses could no longer be hidden, his mother placed him in a basket to float down the Nile. Pharaoh's daughter, bathing nearby in the river, saw the basket and decided to raise the baby as her own.[4]

When Moses grew up and understood his Israelite heritage, he was troubled at the injustice suffered by his people. One day he killed an Egyptian who was beating a Hebrew slave. Moses thought his act had been done in secret, but Pharaoh soon learned what had happened and Moses was forced to run for his life.[5]

---

[1] Exodus 1:6-10
[2] Exodus 1:11-14
[3] Exodus 1:15-22
[4] Exodus 2:1-10
[5] Exodus 2:11-15

Moses ended up in Midian and started a new life there. In his absence, the oppression of the Israelites by a new Pharaoh grew even worse. God heard their cries and determined that the time was right for another new beginning, this one to be carried out by Moses.[6]

God's choice of a deliverer was hard to understand. Moses had never lived with his own people except as an infant, and his attempts to help his people had not gone well. As an 80-year-old foreigner living in Midian, he no longer had any connection with his own people and no influence with their oppressors. In spite of all these shortcomings, Moses was God's clear choice.[7]

The call of Moses began with a burning bush on a mountainside. When Moses went over for a closer look, | 2 |
God called him by name and told him to take off his sandals because he was standing on holy ground. God's message was simple: "I have heard the cries of my people suffering at the hands of the Egyptians and I am sending you to bring them out of Egypt and into the Land I promised to their ancestors."[8]

As Moses listened to what God was saying, he was plagued with self-doubts:

- Who am I to do such a thing?[9]

- If I go to the Israelites, who shall I say sent me?[10]

- What if they refuse to believe me?[11]

- Given how poorly I speak, who would listen?[12]

God responded to each of these objections raised by Moses:

---

[6] Exodus 2:16-25

[7] Exodus 7:7

[8] Exodus 3:6-10

[9] Exodus 3:11

[10] Exodus 3:13

[11] Exodus 4:1

[12] Exodus 4:10

- How will you do this? I will be with you every step of the way.[13]

- Who am I? I am who I am, the LORD, the God of Abraham, Isaac and Jacob.[14]

- The Israelites will believe you and eventually Pharaoh will as well. Why? Because my power will be with you, making it possible for you to perform signs and wonders.[15]

- How will you know what to say? I will give you every word.[16]

3   Even with all these assurances, Moses asked God to send someone else. God was not pleased with such a response, but came up with a plan that overcame this final objection: God would tell Moses what to say, Moses would tell his brother, Aaron, and Aaron would speak to the Israelites and Pharaoh.[17]

Fresh out of excuses, Moses reluctantly returned to Egypt and with Aaron's assistance, told the Israelites what God had said. Moses was somewhat shocked that the Israelites actually believed him, but they were ready to hear God was concerned about their suffering and would do something on their behalf.[18]

The confrontation with Pharaoh began with Aaron bringing a simple message from the LORD: *Let my people go.* Pharaoh's response was dismissive, saying that he neither knew nor feared such a god and would never consider letting his slaves leave the country for any reason. Thinking the slaves were rebelling because they had it too easy, Pharaoh decided that making them work harder would put an end to such foolishness. He stopped supplying straw for making bricks, and required the Israelites to

---

[13] Exodus 3:12

[14] Exodus 3:14-17

[15] Exodus 3:18-20; 4:2-9

[16] Exodus 4:12

[17] Exodus 4:13-16

[18] Exodus 4:19-31

find their own straw and make the same number of bricks as always. They complained that this was impossible. Pharaoh told them they were just lazy.[19]

Needless to say, this development left the Israelites unhappy. They complained to Moses and Moses complained to God, who reassured him that the hardness of Pharaoh's heart would provide the right context for Israel's deliverance. God told Moses to tell the Israelites:

> I am the LORD! And with my mighty power I will punish the Egyptians and free you from slavery. I will accept you as my people, and I will be your God. Then you will know that I was the one who rescued you from the Egyptians. I will bring you into the land that I solemnly promised Abraham, Isaac, and Jacob, and it will be yours. I am the LORD![20]

The Israelites were too discouraged to find much hope in such a message, and Moses was again filled with doubt: if his own people scoffed at his message, how could he ever convince Pharaoh? Even so, Moses went back to Pharaoh, who told him to do a miracle to prove God's power. Aaron threw his staff on the ground and it became a snake, but Pharaoh's magicians were able to do the same. Pharaoh was unimpressed even when Aaron's snake ate up the other snakes. The time was at hand for God's power to be displayed through devastating plagues.[21]

The first plague: Blood. Moses and Aaron went to Pharaoh again with God's demand: *Let my people go*! Pharaoh refused and Moses struck the water of the Nile with his staff and the river turned to blood, killing all the fish within it. Because his magicians were once again able to duplicate this feat, Pharaoh

---

[19] Exodus 5:1-18
[20] Exodus 5:20-21; 6:6-8 (CEV)
[21] Exodus 6:9-12; 7:8-13

remained unimpressed.[22]

The second plague: Frogs. Moses returned to Pharaoh and warned him that if the Israelites were not allowed to leave the country to worship their god in the wilderness, frogs would multiply and overrun the land. Pharaoh promised to let the Israelites worship as they wanted, but only in Egypt and only if the plague ended. When it did, Pharaoh changed his mind.[23]

The third plague: Gnats. Moses and Aaron came to Pharaoh saying, *Let my people go*, and warning of a plague of gnats throughout the land. Pharaoh's magicians, unable to duplicate this plague as they had the first two, told Pharaoh, "This is done by the hand of God." Pharaoh was not convinced.[24]

The fourth plague: Flies. When Moses and Aaron returned to Pharaoh again, the demand was the same, *Let my people go*, but the warning was different. The next plague would affect the Egyptians, but not the Israelites. In the midst of the plague, Pharaoh again promised to let the Israelites go, but only if they stayed nearby. When the plague was lifted, Pharaoh refused to honor his promise.[25]

The fifth plague: Livestock. Since Pharaoh refused to let God's people go, another plague ensued, this time killing the Egyptian horses, donkeys, camels, cattle, sheep and goats. Though Pharaoh saw how the plague spared the Israelites while devastating the Egyptians, his heart was unyielding.[26]

The sixth plague: Boils. Moses and Aaron came before Pharaoh and threw ashes in the air that became boils wherever they landed on people and animals. The boils were so painful that Pharaoh's magicians could not even appear in his presence.

---

[22] Exodus 7:14-24

[23] Exodus 8:1-15

[24] Exodus 8:16-19

[25] Exodus 8:20-32

[26] Exodus 9:1-7

Nevertheless, Pharaoh's resolve never wavered.[27]

The seventh plague: Hail. Moses and Aaron now told Pharaoh that the LORD's power would be revealed in an even greater way if Pharaoh did not let the Israelites go: hailstorms would be so intense that they would kill every living thing that had not found shelter. The storm came as predicted and, though the Israelites were spared, the destruction throughout the rest of Egypt was unprecedented. Pharaoh took notice and admitted to Moses that he had been wrong not to let the Israelites go worship their god. He said that if Moses would stop the hail, the people could go. When the hail stopped, Pharaoh once again changed his mind.[28]

The eighth plague: Locusts. Moses and Aaron confronted Pharaoh with his arrogance and warned that a coming swarm of locusts would be so great that everything not already destroyed by the hail would be gone. Pharaoh said the Israelite men could go and worship, but insisted the women and children remain behind. Because such a compromise failed to meet God's demands, the locusts came and devoured everything.[29]

The ninth plague: Darkness. This time, the plague began even before Moses and Aaron went to Pharaoh. Except for the areas where the Israelites lived, darkness covered all of Egypt for three days. Pharaoh summoned Moses and told him all the Israelites – men, women and children – could go into the wilderness to worship their god, but all their flocks and herds must be left behind. Moses refused, saying they would not know what animals to sacrifice until they arrived at their destination. Pharaoh was enraged and told Moses and Aaron never to appear in his presence again or they would be killed on the spot. Moses responded, "So be it!"[30]

The tenth plague: Death of the Firstborn. The LORD told

---

[27] Exodus 9:8-12
[28] Exodus 9:13-35
[29] Exodus 10:1-20
[30] Exodus 10:21-29

Moses that there would be a final plague, one so devastating in its impact that Pharaoh would not only allow the Israelites to leave, but would insist they do so. Having ordered the death of every son born to the Israelites, Pharaoh would now see the death of every firstborn son in Egypt, including his own. This plague would pass over the Israelites, showing Pharaoh that the LORD indeed had a special relationship with them.[31]

In order for the Israelites to be spared this final plague, each family would have to follow strict instructions. They were to take one of their best lambs or goats and slaughter it at twilight, putting the animal's blood on the doorframes of each house.[32]

5 | Inside each house, families would have a special meal of bitter herbs, bread made without yeast, and roasted meat of the sacrificed animal. Everything would be eaten in haste, with every person dressed and ready to leave. This meal would be called *Passover* because of what God had promised:

> *On that night I will pass through the land of Egypt and strike down every firstborn son and firstborn male animal in the land of Egypt. I will execute judgment against all the gods of Egypt, for I am the LORD! But the blood on your doorposts will serve as a sign, marking the houses where you are staying. When I see the blood, I will pass over you. This plague of death will not touch you when I strike the land of Egypt.*[33]

Moses told the Israelites the Passover meal was to be celebrated for all generations to come. Eating bread made without yeast would be a lasting reminder of the urgency with which they left their bondage in Egypt.[34]

When the death of the firstborn happened in the middle of the night, there was loud wailing in Pharaoh's palace and throughout

---

[31] Exodus 11:1-8

[32] Exodus 12:1-7

[33] Exodus 12:12-13 (NLT)

[34] Exodus 12:14-20; 12:43-49

Egypt. That very night, Pharaoh ordered the Israelites to take everything that belonged to them and leave his country immediately, lest the plagues continue and every Egyptian die. The Israelites were fully prepared, and on their way out of the country asked for and were given silver and gold from many families anxious to be rid of this troublesome people at all cost.[35]

Moses took with him the bones of Jacob. Though more than 400 years had passed since Jacob's death, the Israelites remembered he had made their ancestors swear an oath to carry his bones with them when God took them back to Canaan.[36]

The Israelites didn't follow the most direct path out of Egypt, but went wherever God led them. It was not difficult to know where to go: God led them by a pillar of fire at night and a pillar of cloud during the day. When they reached the edge of the sea, God told them to camp there.[37]

Back in Egypt, Pharaoh was thinking about what had happened. He became increasingly angry that he had given in to the pressures put on him, and been made to look weak by letting part of his workforce leave. It wasn't long before Pharaoh decided to pursue the Israelites and force them to return.[38]

The Israelites were terrified when they saw the approaching army. They complained to Moses that it would have been better to live in Egypt as slaves than to die as free people in the desert. Moses tried to reassure them: if they would only be patient, they would be saved by the LORD.[39]

God told Moses to stretch out his staff over the sea. All night a powerful wind blew and the waters gradually | 6 | parted. The Israelites marched through on dry ground the next morning, but when the Egyptians tried to follow, it was a

---

[35] Exodus 12:29-36

[36] Exodus 13:19

[37] Exodus 13:17-22; 14:1-2

[38] Exodus 14:5-9

[39] Exodus 14:10-14

different story. Moses stretched out his staff over the sea once again and the waters returned, drowning Pharaoh and his army in the process.[40]

The Israelites stood in awe at what had happened. They were finally ready to worship the LORD, who had delivered them from the mighty Egyptians. Moses and his sister, Miriam, led the Israelites in a new song:

> *I sing praises to the LORD for his great victory!*
> > *He has thrown the horses and their riders into the sea.*
> *The LORD is my strength, the reason for my song,*
> > *because he has saved me.*
> *I praise and honor the LORD--*
> > *he is my God and the God of my ancestors.*
> *The LORD is his name, and he is a warrior!* [41]

---

[40] Exodus 14:15-28
[41] Exodus 14:31; 15:1-3 (CEV)

Questions for Reflection/Discussion

1. Pharaoh's decree to kill the newborn Hebrew males meant that he was willing to sacrifice his future workforce for the sake of his present security. How have today's business or political leaders put the future at risk for the sake of the present?

2. God heard the cries of the Hebrew slaves and responded by calling Moses to be their deliverer. Do you find it comforting that God acted in response to those who were being treated so cruelly, or do you find yourself troubled that others have been abused with no one being sent by God to deliver them? Do you think that some may have been called by God to be deliverers, but refused to listen or respond?

3. This story describes the struggle between the reluctance of Moses and the patient determination of God. Have you ever been reluctant to do something that you knew you were supposed to do? What happened?

4. The discouragement of the mistreated Hebrew slaves was so great that they had trouble hearing God's message to them through Moses. Have you ever been so discouraged that you've had a hard time hearing words of hope and encouragement? How and when did things change for you?

5. The Passover meal involved special foods that reminded the Hebrews of what God had done for them. What meals or foods have special significance for your family? Are these connected to God in any way?

6. The Israelites felt hopeless when they were trapped between the Egyptian army and the sea, but God made a way for them. Have you ever felt trapped and hopeless? What happened next?

CHAPTER 4:
LESSONS IN THE DESERT

1   It was not long before the joy of escaping Pharaoh's army gave way to the problems of living in the desert. The scarcity of food and water led to a recurring complaint against God and Moses: "Did you bring us into the desert to make us suffer and die? Life in Egypt was better than this!"[1]

God told the Israelites their needs would be met. That evening, huge flocks of quail appeared and were easily captured. The next morning, thin flakes that looked like frost appeared on the ground. This manna, which tasted like wafers made with honey, was unlike anything the Israelites had ever seen. God gave them clear instructions about it:

1. Collect only as much as you need for each day.

2. Collect each Friday as much as you need for two days.

3. Collect nothing on Saturday because that is the Sabbath.[2]

These instructions were simple enough, but people still had trouble following them. Those who thought it made sense to collect extra each day to prepare for the future found their surplus spoiled. Those who failed to collect extra on Friday were dismayed when there was no manna on Saturday. Eventually people discovered it was best to follow God's instructions.[3]

The Israelites were not able to find a place in the desert that had adequate supplies of water. When what they had was gone, they accused Moses again of bringing them into the desert just to make them suffer and die. God told Moses to take his staff and strike a large rock. When he did, water came rushing out, and the

---

[1] Exodus 15:22-27; 16:1-3

[2] Exodus 16:4-5; 16:13-14; 16:31

[3] Exodus 16:19-30

people had all they needed.[4]

Three months into their journey, the Israelites came to Mt Sinai and camped there. God gave Moses a message for the Israelites: "If you obey me and keep my covenant, then you will be my treasured people out of all the nations on earth." When Moses told them what God had said, the Israelites responded with a resounding "Yes!" He told them to prepare themselves for entering into this covenant with the LORD by bathing, washing their clothes, and abstaining from sex for three days.[5]

The Ten Commandments

On the third day, the LORD's presence enveloped the mountain in smoke and fire. At God's invitation, Moses and Aaron went up the mountain. Over the next forty days Moses received stone tablets with commandments inscribed on them:[6]

1. Don't let anything become more important to you than this: I am the LORD your God, the One who gave you life and the One who gave you freedom.

2. Don't try to make anything that looks like me, and don't worship anything that others say looks like me.

3. Don't use my name when you want to vent your anger or justify your actions.

4. Don't become so busy that you have no time for me; one day a week should be set aside as a Sabbath for renewal and remembrance.

5. Treat your parents with the respect they deserve.

6. Don't put an end to the life I have given anyone.

7. Don't seek to satisfy your sexual desires outside the bonds of marriage.

8. Don't take for yourself anything that belongs to others.

9. Don't get others in trouble by telling lies about them.

---

[4] Exodus 17:1-7
[5] Exodus 19:5-15
[6] Exodus 19:16-24; 24:12-18

10. Don't obsess about having what others have.[7]

Beyond the Ten Commandments

Many other laws that dealt with specific situations were added to these ten basic ones. Those who knew (or should have known) their actions would cause harm, were to be held accountable. Their punishment was to be proportional (an eye for an eye), not excessive. The testimony of one person would never be enough to put anyone to death. [8]

2 Murder and kidnapping carried the death penalty, but so did working on the Sabbath or any physical or verbal attack on parents. Sorcerers, mediums, spiritists, those who had sex with animals, and those who worshiped false gods were to be put to death. Those who had sex with someone of their own gender or with someone married or betrothed to another person were to be executed as well.[9]

Special consideration was to be given to those who were poor, especially widows, orphans and foreigners. Those who lent money were not to charge interest, but were to be governed by compassion for those in need. The rights of the poor and powerless were to be guarded when conflicts arose with the rich and powerful.[10]

The rights of slaves were to be maintained. Those who were unable to pay their debts were to be set free after six years of being bondservants regardless of how much they still owed. Slave families were to be kept together, and escaped slaves were not to be returned to their masters.[11]

Life was to have a balance of work and rest. Crops were to be

---

[7] Exodus 20:2-17; Deuteronomy 5:6-21

[8] Exodus 21:28 – 22:15; Numbers 25:30; Deuteronomy 17:2-7; 19:15

[9] Exodus 31:15; 21:12-27; 22:18-20; Leviticus 20:27; 20:10-14;
    Numbers 15:32-36; Deuteronomy 22:23-29

[10] Exodus 22:21-27; 23:6-9;Deuteronomy 24:10-13; 24:17-22

[11] Exodus 21:2-11; Deuteronomy 23:15-16

harvested for six years; the seventh year was to be made holy by letting poor people and wild animals gather from the fields whatever they could. Six days of work would be sufficient for each week; the seventh day would be a Sabbath, not only for owners to rest, but for their slaves and animals to rest as well.[12]

Those who found lost items were obligated to return them to their rightful owners. Honor and integrity were to be maintained at all costs, even when it meant siding with those who were reviled.[13]

God was to be honored by three festivals each year. Passover would celebrate the deliverance of the Israelites from slavery in Egypt. Other festivals would celebrate the beginning and ending of harvest. Each festival was to be celebrated in a way that was fitting and appropriate.[14]

Some of these laws were effective immediately; others were to be implemented when they reached Canaan, the Land promised to Abraham, Isaac and Jacob. God told the Israelites that their journey would be long and hard, but if they remained faithful to their covenant with the LORD, their needs would be met and their enemies defeated. Tassels on the bottom of their garments would be a constant reminder to the Israelites of this covenant.[15]

The Tabernacle

Because the Israelites were on a journey, God gave Moses the design of a worship center that could be easily moved. They were to donate their treasures for the Tabernacle's construction, but only as their heart prompted them; building a dwelling place for God was to be considered a privilege, not a burden.[16]

The Tabernacle was to include a covered tent and an open courtyard. The materials used to make the Tabernacle were to be

---

[12] Exodus 23:10-13;

[13] Exodus 23:1-9

[14] Exodus 23:14-19; Leviticus 23:1-44

[15] Exodus 23:20-33; Numbers 15:37-41

[16] Exodus 25:1-8

extravagant, bringing vivid colors and luxurious textures together in ways appropriate for a place of holy mystery.[17]

Within the covered tent would be two rooms. The outer room would have a small table overlaid with gold and a solid gold Menorah, a stand holding seven lamps. The inner room, the Holy of Holies, would contain the Ark of the Covenant and mercy seat. The Ark, a box four feet long and three feet wide overlaid with gold, would contain the stone tablets of the Ten Commandments. The mercy seat, placed on top of the ark and overlaid with gold, would have images of angels facing each other. In addition to its function as a cover for the Ark, the mercy seat would be a symbolic throne for God. The open courtyard would have an altar for burnt sacrifices and a lamp that would remain lit every night for generations to come.[18]

The Tabernacle and all its furnishings would be maintained by Aaron and his sons. The high priest, the only person ever to enter the Holy of Holies, would wear clothing of elaborate design incorporating not only the finest fabrics, but also costly gemstones on which would be inscribed the names of Israel's twelve tribes. The hem of his robe would be adorned with bells to signal his entrance and exit.[19]

Priests were to be held to a higher standard of holiness. They were not to shave their heads, trim their beards or tattoo their bodies. They could be married, but not to any woman who had been a prostitute or divorced. No priest who had a physical handicap could approach the altar to offer sacrifices.[20]

A special weeklong service of consecration would set apart the priests for their special duty. This would be done by having the priests each day put on their special garments and be anointed

---

[17] Exodus 26:1-36

[18] Exodus 25:10-40; 26:33-34; 27:1-21

[19] Exodus 28:1-43

[20] Leviticus 21:5-23

with olive oil and the blood of a ram.[21]

The Tabernacle would be consecrated by anointing it with oil and perfumes; the altar for burnt offerings would be consecrated in seven days of sacrifices. From then on, two lambs would be sacrificed every morning and evening.[22]

The Golden Bull

While Moses was on the mountain receiving these instructions about how the Israelites were to live in covenant with the LORD, the people were growing desperate in the valley below. Fearing that something had happened to Moses, they turned to Aaron, the only person they thought could take his place. They asked Aaron to make an idol that would reconnect them with God.[23]

Aaron, having no message from God to the contrary, granted their request. They gave him all their gold jewelry and he melted and molded it into the shape of a bull. When the people saw the golden idol, they shouted, "This is the god who brought us out of Egypt." Aaron then built an altar for sacrifices and proclaimed a festival of celebration. The festival began with burnt sacrifices and other offerings, continued with much eating and drinking, and eventually became a drunken orgy.[24]

Back on the mountain, God knew what the Israelites were doing and told Moses that it would be better to destroy them all and start over. Moses pleaded for his people, saying that destroying them would make God look foolish in the eyes of the Egyptians. Moses asked God to forgive the people if for no other reason than for the sake of promises made to Abraham, Isaac and Jacob. God agreed to do so.[25]

As Moses came down the mountain, he heard noises coming from the Israelite camp. When he was close enough to see the

---

[21] Exodus 29:1-36; Leviticus 6:8 – 9:24
[22] Exodus 30:22-29; 29:37-46
[23] Exodus 32:1
[24] Exodus 32:2-6
[25] Exodus 32:7-13

people dancing around their golden idol, Moses became so angry that he threw down the stone tablets, breaking them into pieces. Then he ground up the golden idol, threw the dust in the water and made everyone celebrating the golden calf drink it.[26]

When asked how he could make such an idol, Aaron blamed the Israelites for being perverse. Moses saw that Aaron had lost control of the people, and decided something drastic needed to be done. He shouted, "Whoever is for the LORD, come to me!" and men from the tribe of Levi responded. He sent them throughout the camp killing all who had rebelled. From this time on, the Levites were set apart as being dedicated to God, with responsibility to maintain the Tabernacle and to assist the priests in whatever ways were needed.[27]

God told Moses to climb Mt. Sinai again for further instructions and a new copy of the Ten Commandments. After forty more days on the mountain, Moses was told to lead the Israelites to the Promised Land. God would not be a constant presence in their midst because that would be disastrous if the Israelites continued to rebel, but would come to them as needed. God would guide Moses and drive out the nations living in the Land.[28]

When Moses came down the mountain, his face glowed from having been with God. This frightened the people, but he reassured them and told them everything God expected of them. The Israelites declared their intention to be God's people by shouting, "We will do everything the LORD has said; we will obey." To confirm this special relationship between God and the Israelites, Moses sacrificed several young bulls and sprinkled their blood on the people, saying, "This is the blood of the covenant that the LORD has made with you."[29]

Because the people were ready to obey and anxious to have a place of worship, they soon began bringing the items that would

---

[26] Exodus 32:14-20

[27] Exodus 32:21-29; Numbers 3:5-38; 4:1-49

[28] Exodus 33:1-11; Exodus 34:1-28

[29] Exodus 24:3-8; Exodus 34:29-32

be needed to construct and furnish the Tabernacle. Before long they had more than enough and the work began.[30]

When the work was finished, Moses examined it and pronounced a blessing on them because everything had been done according to God's instructions. The LORD's presence filled the Tabernacle and not even Moses dared enter it. From then on, the Israelites traveled whenever the cloud of God's presence lifted from the Tabernacle to guide them.[31]

Tabernacle Offerings

Now that the Tabernacle was in place, a system of offerings was instituted. Since the beginning of time, burnt sacrifices had been a common practice of all religions, but from now on, offerings to God were to conform to strict regulations. Most importantly, offerings were to take place at the Tabernacle, where God's presence dwelt; anyone offering sacrifices in any other place or to any other god was to be excluded from the community.[32]

The *Whole Burnt Offering* was to atone for sin, restoring a person's relationship with God after it had been severed by breaking one of God's commandments. Such atonement covered unintentional wrongdoing only; anyone who showed disregard for God by sinning defiantly was considered beyond forgiveness. Atonement offerings followed a specific procedure:[33]

1. The *presentation* of an animal from a herd or flock; wild or captured animals were not acceptable because they would cost the person nothing; defective animals were considered unworthy sacrifices.

2. The *laying on of hands* to connect the owner to the animal, "transferring" the person's sins in the process.

3. The *slaughter* of the animal by cutting its throat and

---

[30] Exodus 35:1-29; 36:2-7

[31] Exodus 39:42-43; 40:34-38

[32] Genesis 4:3-5; Leviticus 1:1; 17:1-9

[33] Numbers 15:22-31

removing its skin and intestines.

4. The *sprinkling of blood* on the altar by the priest.

5. The *burning of the remains* on the altar by the priest, who could keep only the animal's skin for himself.[34]

The **Sin Offering** brought purification for offenses committed by priests, leaders and the congregation as a whole. This offering began the same, but the blood was not sprinkled on the altar and only the choicest part of the animal was burned on the altar; the remainder was burned outside the camp.[35]

The **Guilt Offering** was required for anyone gaining property improperly through fraud or force. Full restitution had to be made to the offended party in addition to a sacrificial offering.[36]

The **Fellowship Offering** was an expression of thanksgiving to God for peace and prosperity. The choicest part of the animal was burned on the altar and a portion was given to the priests; the rest was eaten by family and friends feasting nearby.[37]

The **Grain Offering** was the only offering that did not involve animal sacrifice. It was an expression of thanksgiving for the fruit of the land. The wheat was ground and sifted to make the finest flour. Olive oil, incense, salt and other ingredients were added if desired, but never yeast or honey. The offering was given to the priests, who burned part of it and ate the rest.[38]

Holiness

Living in covenant with God was a privilege, but it carried ethical expectations as well. Moses explained to the Israelites that such behavior was at the heart of being the people of God:

I am the LORD who brought you up out of Egypt to be

---

[34] Leviticus 1:2-17; 7:8; 22:17-25

[35] Leviticus 4:1 – 5:13

[36] Leviticus 5:14 – 6:7

[37] Leviticus 3:1-17; 19:5-8

[38] Leviticus 2:1-16; 6:15-16

your God; you must be holy because I am holy.[39]

To be holy meant to be set apart as something dedicated to God and special. Regulations concerning holiness were given in regard to almost every area of life. Those who violated the regulations were excluded from the community of faith until they could be restored through burnt offerings.[40]

3

God told Moses what could be eaten: animals who had split hoofs and chewed their cud (cattle, sheep and goats); water creatures who had fins and scales (virtually all fish); birds who were not flesh-eating (quail, pigeons, turkeys, and many more); and a few specific insects (locusts, crickets and grasshoppers). God also told Moses what was "unclean" and not to be eaten: camels, rabbits, pigs, shrimp, lobsters, crabs, all birds of prey and most insects.[41]

4

Eating any of the unclean foods (or even touching them) made a person unclean. Animals killed in the wild were unclean unless the blood was drained from them before the meat was eaten. Blood was sacred, both because life was in the blood and because blood was the means of atoning for sin.[42]

Women were made unclean by menstruating or giving birth, but could be cleansed by a burnt sacrifice of a lamb or dove. Men who were made unclean by any discharge of semen could be cleansed by washing, but if the discharge was from a sexually transmitted disease, it would be necessary to present a burnt offering seven days after the discharge ceased.[43]

Anyone having a rash, boil, sore, or any other skin disease was unclean and required to come before a priest for an initial inspection and then a follow-up seven days later. Unless the priest pronounced such people cured, they were required to

---

[39] Leviticus 11:45
[40] Leviticus 19:1-37
[41] Leviticus 11:1-23
[42] Leviticus 11:24-27; 17:10-14
[43] Leviticus 12:1-8; 15:19-30; 15:1-18

separate themselves from others, dress in rags, wear masks and shout "Unclean! Unclean!" when anyone came near. If the priest pronounced them cured, they were to be sprinkled seven times with a dove dipped in the blood of a second dove. The live dove was then to be released.[44]

It was not only people who could become ritually unclean, but clothing and homes as well. If mold, mildew or any fungal growth was found on an item, it was to be examined by a priest, scraped and washed, then re-examined by the priest seven days later. If the problem remained, the item was to be burned.[45]

The Israelites were not to follow the sexual practices prevalent where they had been (Egypt) or where they were going (Canaan). Sex was forbidden with neighbors and close relatives (a man was not to have sex with his mother, stepmother, mother-in-law, aunt, niece, daughter, daughter-in-law, sister, sister-in-law or half-sister, for example). Sex with different generations (a man having sex with both a mother and her daughter, for example) was forbidden. Sex with a person of the same gender was forbidden, as was sex with animals. Children were not to be offered as burnt sacrifices.[46]

Holy Days

Because God rested on the seventh day after six days of creation, the Sabbath was sacred. Saturday was to be a day of rest and sacred assembly, not a day of work. Every seventh year was to be a Sabbath in which the land itself would be at rest. During the Sabbath year, no work was to be done in planting or tending the fields, but whatever grew freely could be harvested and used.[47]

After seven Sabbath years had passed, the fiftieth year would be a year of Jubilee. All debts were to be canceled and all land that had been sold was to be returned to its original owner. Any

---

[44] Leviticus 13:1-45; 14:1-32

[45] Leviticus 13:47-59; 14:33-53

[46] Leviticus 18:1-28

[47] Leviticus 23:3; 25:1-7

Israelite who had become a slave to pay off debt was to be set free; only foreigners could be slaves for life.[48]

Individuals who violated these laws brought shame and guilt not only on themselves, but on the entire community for having failed to live according to God's standards. This communal guilt required a Day of Atonement, the one day each year when the high priest was allowed to enter the Tabernacle's Holy of Holies. He was to present a bull as a burnt offering for his own sins first. Then he was to remove his priestly garments, bathe and put on linen clothing that was simple and sacred. Only then would he be ready to enter the Holy of Holies. The priests learned the hard way that any who disregarded such instructions met dire consequences.[49]

The high priest would atone for the sins of the people by choosing two goats. One would be sacrificed as a burnt offering and its blood sprinkled on the altar. The other goat, the scapegoat, would be sent into the wilderness after the high priest had laid hands on the goat's head and recited the sins of the people over it.[50]

The Covenant

God told Moses that if the Israelites would conform to these ethical and religious requirements, they would be blessed with unending peace and prosperity. Breaking the covenant, however, would bring misery in many forms: plague, famine, drought, and defeat by enemies. Even then, God would forgive the people if they turned from their evil ways and embraced the covenant once again.[51]

Moses gave all these instructions to the Israelites and said that what was being asked of them was within their reach | 5 | if they would only take God's words into their hearts and

---

[48] Leviticus 25:1-55

[49] Leviticus 16:1-6; 10:1-7

[50] Leviticus 16:5-28

[51] Leviticus 26:3-45

remember them. Moses emphasized that this was a matter of life and death: following God's instructions would bring them a good life that was blessed in every way; turning away from the LORD's instructions to follow other gods or the inclinations of their own hearts would bring death and destruction. Moses summed it all up like this:

> *This day I call the heavens and the earth as witnesses against you that I have set before you life and death, blessings and curses. Now choose life, so that you and your children may live and that you may love the LORD your God, listen to his voice, and hold fast to him. For the LORD is your life, and he will give you many years in the land he swore to give to your fathers, Abraham, Isaac and Jacob.* [52]

---

[52] Deuteronomy 30:19-20 (TNIV)

Questions for Reflection/Discussion

1. Problems in the desert made the Israelites long for the good old days back in Egypt. When people today long for the good old days, what is it they feel has been lost? What things from today might we miss the most if we turned back the clock to a time long ago?

2. The Ten Commandments say we are not to kill anyone, and yet other commandments carry a death penalty. How do we decide what to do if commandments differ from each other? Adultery and homosexual activity both carry the death penalty. Why do you think so many Christians today seem far more tolerant of those who commit adultery than they do of those who engage in homosexual activity?

3. Holiness is defined here as "set apart as something dedicated to God and special." Some today define holiness by things we should do (go to church, read the Bible, etc.) and things we should not do (drink, smoke, dance, gamble, etc.). How are these definitions of holiness similar or different? What do you think it should mean to live a holy life today?

4. This chapter defines certain foods and other things as being unclean. Scholars have come up with explanations why some things are on this list, but other items remain a mystery. What foods are acceptable today in some cultures, but detestable in others? What activities, encounters or experiences in our own day might leave someone feeling unclean?

5. Moses says God gave the Israelites the same choice Adam and Eve had: life through obedience or death through rebellion. What self-destructive behaviors do people choose today? Why do people have trouble making good choices?

CHAPTER 5:
CONQUERING CANAAN

After the Israelites had affirmed their covenant with God, and the Tabernacle had been built and consecrated, God told Moses to take a census of the men old enough to be soldiers. As the Israelites resumed their journey to Canaan, the Promised Land, three tribes marched on each side of the Tabernacle (north, south, east and west) throughout the journey.[1]

Each day as their journey began and the Ark of the Covenant was moved, Moses shouted:

> *Rise up, O Lord! May your enemies be scattered;*
> *May those who hate you flee in terror!*

And when the day's journey ended and the Ark of the Covenant came to rest, Moses shouted:

> *Return, O Lord, to the midst of your people.*[2]

1 The journey was both difficult and monotonous. The people ate only manna day after day and longed for the foods they had back in Egypt. They complained constantly to Moses, who told God the burden of leading the people was too much for him. God consecrated seventy people who would assist Moses as elders, and then sent flocks of quail to give the Israelites a change of diet. Many ate so greedily that they became sick and died.[3]

As the Israelites approached Canaan, God told Moses to send one man from each tribe to explore the Promised Land. The men returned after forty days with a mixed report: the Land was good, flowing with milk and honey, but the people were large and powerful. "We looked like grasshoppers to them," the men said.[4]

---

[1] Numbers 1:1 – 2:34

[2] Numbers 10:35-36

[3] Numbers 11:1-35

[4] Numbers 13:1-33

Joshua and Caleb tried to convince the Israelites that God would give them victory, but the people grumbled that they should have stayed in Egypt. When the people wanted to kill Joshua and Caleb, God's anger burned against them: "How long will these people treat me with contempt? How long will they refuse to believe in spite of all the miraculous signs I have shown them?"[5]

Moses appealed to God's sense of justice and mercy, and God decided that some Israelites should enter the Land, | 2 |
but not those who had shown such contempt. They would wander in the desert for forty years, one year for each of the days the men had explored the Land. By then this faithless generation would have passed away, and a new generation would have taken its place.[6]

When the people heard this message, they said they now realized the error of their ways and would enter the Land to do battle with whoever lived there. Moses warned them that this was yet another example of their failure to listen to God. Refusing to listen to Moses, they mounted an attack, were soundly defeated, and retreated to the wilderness.[7]

The wilderness years were difficult, with dissatisfaction at every turn. The Levites complained about not being priests, and God reaffirmed that only Aaron and his descendants were to fill that role. People grumbled that Moses and Aaron had too much power, and God dealt with the complainers harshly.[8]

The people complained about the lack of water and God told Moses to gather the people and command water to come out of the rock. Moses angrily denounced the Israelites as rebels, and struck the rock to bring forth water. When nothing happened, he struck the rock again. God was upset with Moses because such a display of temper was a poor way to honor God. Moses was told he would bring the Israelites to the Land, but would not enter

---

[5] Numbers 14:1-12
[6] Numbers 14:20-35
[7] Numbers 14:40-45
[8] Numbers 16:1 – 18:32

with them.[9]

Before long, the people complained again about the lack of food and water. This time, God's punishment came in the form of poisonous snakes. The people realized they had sinned against God and prayed for deliverance. God told Moses to put one of the snakes on a pole and lift it up. Those who looked upon the snake after having been bitten were healed.[10]

Eventually the Israelites encountered the Ammonites, Edomites and Moabites. Because these people were descendants of Jacob's brother, Esau, and Abraham's nephew, Lot, the Israelites were told they should not attempt to defeat them or take their land or possessions. As they approached each country, the Israelites asked permission to pass through. Although they assured each king they intended no harm, their words were often met with skepticism by those who decided the safest course of action was to attack the Israelites. As God granted victory to the Israelites in each of these encounters, their reputation grew.[11]

3 By the time the Israelites reached Moab, its inhabitants trembled with fear. Their king sent for Balaam, hoping this prophet would pronounce a curse on the Israelites. Though Balaam practiced a different religion, he prayed to the LORD and was told the Israelites were a blessed people. When the King of Moab learned of this, he offered to pay a large sum if Balaam would only curse the Israelites as requested. Balaam agreed, and set out on the journey to Moab. On the way, Balaam would have been killed by an angel of God had not his donkey alerted him to the danger. Balaam saw the error of his ways and decided to end his journey, but the angel told him he should go on. Balaam was to be careful, however, to say only what God told him to say.[12]

The King of Moab was delighted to see Balaam, and gave him everything he requested, but was shocked when Balaam's first

---

[9] Numbers 20:2-12

[10] Numbers 21:4-9

[11] Numbers 21:1-3; 21:21-35; Deuteronomy 2:2 – 3:11

[12] Numbers 22:1-35

curse on the Israelites came out as a blessing instead. The same thing happened three more times and the king was furious at what Balaam had done. Balaam responded that he could only say the words God gave him to say. Then Balaam delivered another message from God; this one was a curse on Moab and all the nations that tried to stop the Israelites from entering the Land.[13]

Although the Israelites were not defeated by the King of Moab's army, they were defeated by the Moabites in other ways when some of the Moabite and Midianite women enticed the Israelites into sexual promiscuity and worship of idols. The Israelites who succumbed to such temptations died in a plague.[14]

Moses, knowing that he would not enter the Land, was pleased when God invited him to go up on the mountain for a glimpse of what had been promised to the Israelites for such a long time. God told Moses to anoint Joshua as his successor, and then God gave Moses one final command: destroy the Midianites for leading the Israelites into promiscuity and idol worship.[15]

Now that the Israelites controlled all the land east of the Jordan River, some of the tribes asked if they could stay there. Moses was upset at first, believing these tribes would discourage the others from entering Canaan. But when the tribes making the request vowed to fight alongside the others until the Land was conquered, Moses gave them what they wanted.[16]

Moses said the Levites were not to have any large portions of the Land for their own, but were to be given 48 cities plus the area surrounding each of them. There would be six "cities of refuge" where people could seek sanctuary when pursued by someone who wished to harm them. Moses gave special instructions that the rights of daughters to inherit property should be protected.[17]

---

[13] Numbers 23:1– 24:25

[14] Numbers 25:1-18

[15] Numbers 27:12-23; 31:1-54; Deuteronomy 3:21-29

[16] Numbers 32:1-31; Deuteronomy 3:12-20

[17] Numbers 35:1 – 36:12; Deuteronomy 4:41-43; 19:1-13

As Moses approached his final days, he recounted the wonder of the Israelites being chosen as God's special people, a nation that would triumph over many other nations that were much larger and more powerful. They were never to forget that the LORD is God and there is no other.[18]

4 Moses emphasized that it was not the righteousness of the Israelites that led God to choose them, but the wickedness of other nations that brought their doom. These were nations who sacrificed their children as burnt offerings, practiced divination and sorcery, interpreted omens, engaged in witchcraft, cast spells, and consulted with the dead as spiritists and mediums. The Israelites had proven themselves to be a rebellious people unwilling to submit to God, but they had also shown their willingness to repent and follow God's law. The other nations had become so evil that nothing remained but to destroy them.[19]

Moses warned that prosperity would one day make them forget that it was God who rescued them from Egypt. They must tell their children that their ability to prosper was a gift from God and that it was faithfulness to the Torah that made such prosperity possible.[20]

The words of the Torah were written down and put in the Ark of the Covenant to be kept as a reminder that even though God's wrath would come upon them and they would be taken into captivity, the day would come when God would gather them together again.[21]

Moses had one final message from God: when the Israelites entered Canaan, they were to drive out all the people living there and destroy all their idols and worship sites. Anything thing left behind would lead them astray and bring their destruction.[22]

---

[18] Deuteronomy 4:32-40

[19] Deuteronomy 9:4-7; 18:9-14

[20] Deuteronomy 6:10-25; 8:10-18

[21] Deuteronomy 30:1 – 31:22

[22] Numbers 33:50-56; 7:1-6; 20:16-18

Moses pronounced a blessing on each of the twelve tribes, climbed up the mountain one last time and was gone. The people mourned his death for thirty days and then Joshua became their leader. God told him to be strong and courageous because even though the conquest of the Land would be difficult, God would be with Joshua in the same way that he had been with Moses.[23]

Joshua sent two spies to cross the Jordan River and check out Jericho. They stayed with Rahab, a prostitute, who hid them when the king sent soldiers to kill them. After the soldiers were gone, she told the spies that everyone in Jericho was afraid the city was doomed. She asked that her family be spared when Jericho was destroyed and they agreed to do so if she would tie a red cord to her window to identify her house. The spies returned to Joshua and told him that victory was assured because all Jericho was trembling in fear of them.[24]

God told Joshua that the Israelites would soon see something amazing. The priests were to carry the Ark of the Covenant into the Jordan River. As soon as their feet touched the water, it parted to let them cross on dry land. Joshua told the Israelites that this would be a sure sign to them that God was with them and would guarantee their success.[25]

Crossing the Jordan River and entering the Land of Abraham, Isaac and Jacob was a major event for the Israelites. Each of the twelve tribes took a stone from the river as they crossed it and used them to create a "stones of remembrance" monument. They celebrated Passover and circumcised all the men who had been born in the wilderness during the forty years that had passed since leaving Egypt. God stopped providing manna for them now because they were finally able to eat the fruit of the land.[26]

The typical way of taking a walled city was to cut off all access to it and wait for the people to surrender after their food and

---

[23] Deuteronomy 33:1-29; Joshua 1:1-9

[24] Joshua 2:1-21

[25] Joshua 3:1-17

[26] Joshua 5:2-12

water was gone. God gave Joshua a different plan for taking Jericho. The army, led by the priests carrying the Ark of the Covenant, was to march around the city each day for six days. On the seventh day, they were to march around it seven times, the priests blowing their trumpets each time. Then the people were to give a great shout and the walls of Jericho would fall.[27]

Jericho was to be utterly destroyed with two exceptions: Rahab and her family were to be spared because she had aided the spies; and everything that was silver, gold, iron or bronze was to go into God's treasury. Joshua warned the Israelites not to take any plunder for themselves, but Achan did so anyway.[28]

5 The conquest of Canaan continued with Joshua preparing to take the next city, but this time the Israelites were defeated and forced to retreat. Joshua was distraught until God told him this was their punishment for the disobedience of one man whose sin would be revealed to all. Joshua had the leaders of the tribes come before him and one was selected. Then the clans of that tribe came and one was selected. Then the families of the clan came and one was selected. The men of the family came forward and the guilty one confessed. Achan said he had taken a beautiful robe plus some silver and gold, and buried them beneath his tent. Joshua had the man and his family put to death and everything belonging to them destroyed.[29]

Joshua attacked the city again, this time outwitting the king who had defeated them earlier. Joshua brought a portion of his army to the city and then fled when attacked. The king, hoping to completely destroy the Israelites this time, pursued them with all his men. The portion of Joshua's army that had been left behind destroyed the unguarded city. The king saw the smoke in the distance and returned to his city, but it was too late.[30]

After the battle had ended, Joshua set up an altar and offered

---

[27] Joshua 6:2-5

[28] Joshua 6:17 – 7:1

[29] Joshua 7:1-26

[30] Joshua 8:1-29

burnt sacrifices to God. Then he read from the Torah to his people, reminding them of the LORD's promised blessings and curses.[31]

When word of how the Israelites were destroying cities began to spread, those who lived in Gibeon devised a plan to save their lives. They dressed in old clothes and went to Joshua, telling him they were from a distant country and asking for a peace treaty. Without asking God for guidance, Joshua took them at their word and signed a treaty with them. Three days later he learned who they really were. Rather than go back on his word, Joshua told the Gibeonites that their lives would be spared, but from now on they would be lowly servants of the priests.[32]

Although the Israelites were upset by what the people of Gibeon had done, others were even more upset. Five kings joined forces and attacked Gibeon for refusing to join with them. Joshua's army defended Gibeon and defeated the armies of the other kings. The Israelites knew God was on their side because at one point huge hailstones pummeled the enemy and at another the sun stood still to give the Israelites extra time to fight. After the battle, the Israelites destroyed the cities of the five kings, and then other cities throughout the region.[33]

Other kings in other regions joined forces to wage war against the Israelites, but all were defeated; not one city other than Gibeon sought to make peace. This was all part of God's plan: as had happened with Pharaoh, the Canaanites would be doomed because their hearts were hard and their determination to wage war was unrelenting.[34]

The fighting continued for several years until the conquest of the Promised Land was nearly complete and God told Joshua it was time to distribute regions of the country to each of the tribes. Caleb, one of the original spies sent out by Moses years before,

---

[31] Joshua 8:30-34

[32] Joshua 9:3-27

[33] Joshua 10:1-43

[34] Joshua 11:1-20

asked that his tribe be given the hill country in order to drive out the Canaanites who remained there.[35]

At last, the Israelites were able to settle down after years of wilderness wandering and conquest. Joshua reminded all of them to observe the Torah as given to Moses, and a crisis quickly emerged. The tribes that had been given land on the east side of the Jordan River built an altar nearby for sacrifices. The other tribes of Israel prepared to go to war against them because they were convinced all the Israelites would be punished for God's command that all sacrifices be offered at the Tabernacle.[36]

The tribes that had built the altar said their intentions were being misunderstood. They were not establishing a second center of worship, but only wanted to have a symbolic connection with the tribes on the other side of the river. To prove their case, they asked God to punish them if indeed their intentions were other than they claimed. This explanation satisfied everyone when no punishment came from God.[37]

As the end of Joshua's life came near, he gathered the leaders around him for his parting words. He encouraged them to do two things in order to retain God's blessings and avoid God's wrath:

1. They were to be careful to obey the Torah.

2. They were not to marry any Canaanite or do anything else that would lead to worshiping Canaanite gods.[38]

6 Joshua reminded the Israelites that the LORD had called Abraham and promised him many descendants and the land they were now inhabiting. He told how God had delivered them from slavery in Egypt and had provided for them throughout their journey in the wilderness. He also recounted how their ancestors had repeatedly rebelled against God. Finally Joshua asked the Israelites to choose whether they would serve

---

[35] Joshua 13:1-13; 16:10; 17:14-18; 14:6-14

[36] Joshua 22:1-20

[37] Joshua 22:21-34

[38] Joshua 23:1-16

the LORD or the gods of other nations. The people responded that they would serve the LORD alone, and Joshua set up a stone monument to bear witness to this decision the Israelites made.[39]

---

[39] Joshua 24:1-27

Questions for Reflection/Discussion

1. The Israelites grumbled constantly about the hardships they faced in the wilderness. In what circumstances are you most likely to grumble and complain?

2. It took a new generation to enter the Promised Land because those that had spent their lives as slaves in Egypt found it very difficult to live by faith. What might your generation need to "unlearn" in order to face today's challenges? What lessons has your generation learned that could be helpful?

3. Balaam was of another religion, and yet he prayed to the LORD and he received a message from the LORD. Do you think people of other religions pray to the same God that you do? What has shaped your thinking on this?

4. The Israelites believed God was on their side as they fought against those who were living in Canaan. During what wars have we believed God was on our side because we were righteous and our enemies were evil? During what wars have at least some thought that might not be the case?

5. It strikes us as unfair that so many innocent people were punished by God because of the disobedience of Achan. Do you think society as a whole bears any responsibility when one of us commits sexual assault? Domestic violence? Child Abuse? A hate crime? Armed robbery? Murder?

6. Joshua told the Israelites they would have to decide whether they would serve the LORD or the gods of other nations. Society and religion often pull us in different directions. How have your values and priorities been shaped by each?

CHAPTER 6:
PERIOD OF THE JUDGES

After the death of Joshua, the conquest of Canaan was carried on sporadically. The tribe of Judah defeated King Adonibezek and cut off his thumbs and big toes to render him helpless. He remarked that such a fate was a fitting punishment from God because he had done the same thing to seventy kings, forcing them to pick up scraps from his table in order to survive.[1]

Some of the tribes were determined to drive out those who remained in their areas, but other tribes were less persistent. Eventually God sent a message to the Israelites: "Because you have refused to drive out these people completely, they will continually torment you and lead you astray."[2]

After the generation that entered the Promised Land passed away, other generations arose that cared little about what God had done for their ancestors. The Israelites adopted the local religions and God punished them by letting their enemies oppress them.[3]

From time to time, God would call judges who would lead the Israelites and deliver them from their enemies. For a while things would be better, but then the people would stop paying attention to what the Torah required and they would be overwhelmed by their enemies once again.[4]

The first judge was Othniel. The Israelites cried out to God for help after being oppressed for eight years by the king of Aram, and God's Spirit came upon Othniel. Under his leadership, the enemy was driven from the country, and for a generation the Israelites were at peace.[5]

---

[1] Judges 1:1-7
[2] Judges 1:8 – 2:3
[3] Judges 2:6-15
[4] Judges 2:16-19
[5] Judges 3:7-11

The Israelites again turned from God and fell subject to the king of Moab. After eighteen years of oppression, they cried out to God and were given Ehud, a man who gained victory through subterfuge. He went to the king of Moab to offer tribute and asked for a private audience. When his request was granted and he was alone with the king, Ehud withdrew a hidden dagger and assassinated him. The Moabites were soon defeated by Ehud's army, and the Israelites had peace for two generations.[6]

2 The Israelites again turned from God and came under the power of a Canaanite king whose army was one of the first to have iron chariots. After twenty years of oppression, the Israelites cried out to God, who sent a message to Deborah, a faithful prophetess who was leading the people. She told a man named Barak that God had chosen him to raise a large army and attack the Canaanites. Barak refused to do so until Deborah assured him that she would go with him.[7]

Although Barak was successful in his battle with the Canaanites, Sisera, commander of their army, escaped and sought refuge from someone he thought was an ally. Jael, the wife of the supposed ally, welcomed Sisera into her tent, and then drove a stake through his temple. By the time Barak found him, Sisera was dead. Deborah and Barak composed a song to celebrate God's victory.[8]

In time the Israelites again turned from God and were given into the hands of the Midianites for seven years. Things were so bad that the Israelites fled to the mountains and lived in caves or whatever shelter they could find. The Midianite hordes appeared out of the desert, destroying crops and taking all the sheep and cattle they could find. After hearing the Israelites' pleas, God sent a prophet to say: "When I delivered you from Egypt and from all your oppressors, I warned you not to worship other

---

[6] Judges 3:12-29

[7] Judges 4:1-10

[8] Judges 4:14 – 5:31

gods. But you have not listened to me."[9]

Even so, God came to the aid of the Israelites once again, this time through a most unlikely leader. Gideon was secretly threshing grain in order to avoid detection by the Midianites when an angel came with a strange greeting: "The LORD is with you, mighty warrior!" When Gideon scoffingly replied that God had long ago abandoned them, he was told to go in God's power and save the Israelites.[10]

Needing reassurance that someone as powerless as he was could do such a thing, Gideon asked for a sign from God and put an offering of meat, broth and unleavened bread on a rock. The angel of God touched the offering with his staff and fire from the rock burned up the offering. Gideon was amazed![11]

His first assignment was to tear down his father's altar to Baal. Gideon did so, but under cover of darkness because he was afraid of how people would react. Indeed, when the community figured out who had done this, they demanded that Gideon be handed over and put to death. Gideon's father responded that if Baal were as powerful as they thought, then Baal should punish Gideon himself.[12]

When the Midianite threat became severe, the Spirit of God came upon Gideon and he assembled an army to fight them. Still uncertain that God was truly with him, Gideon asked for a sign. He put a lamb's fleece out at night and asked God to cover the fleece with dew by morning, leaving the ground around it dry. When his request was granted, he was still uncertain and asked the next night that the fleece be dry and the ground covered with dew. This request was granted as well and Gideon was ready.[13]

As Gideon prepared his troops for battle, God told him that the

---

[9] Judges 6:1-10
[10] Judges 6:11-14
[11] Judges 6:15-24
[12] Judges 6:25-32
[13] Judges 6:33-40

army was so large that if they won, they would conclude that it was their own numbers rather than God's power that was responsible. God told Gideon to announce that any soldier who trembled with fear should return home, and more than 20,000 did so. Because the 10,000 that remained were still too many, God said to have the men drink from the stream. Only those who maintained their vigilance while drinking would be ready to fight. Gideon did as God said and ended up with 300 soldiers.[14]

Needing reassurance once again, Gideon was told by God to sneak into the enemy's camp at night and listen to what they were saying. He had no trouble gaining access to the camp because the Midianite army was so large that they feared no ambush. What Gideon heard, though, convinced him that the Midianites were vulnerable. The first soldier he came across was telling another about a terrible dream. The second soldier concluded it was an omen that God was fighting on behalf of Gideon. He said if this was so, the Midianites were doomed.[15]

Gideon was elated by what he heard and returned to his soldiers confident of victory. He told them to shout "For the LORD and for Gideon" as they blew their trumpets and charged the enemy camp. The Midianite army, in total disarray, sought to escape by any means possible. Gideon asked for assistance from other Israelites, but many refused because they feared retribution from the Midianites. When the fighting was over, Gideon confronted the Israelites who failed to assist him earlier. In his rage, Gideon tortured some and killed others.[16]

The Israelites were so impressed by Gideon's victory that they asked him to become their ruler. He responded humbly, "I will not rule over you, nor will my son rule over you. The LORD will rule over you."[17]

Gideon's affirmation of God's reign was soon shown to be

---

[14] Judges 7:1-8

[15] Judges 7:9-15

[16] Judges 7:16-25; 8:1-17

[17] Judges 8:22-23

disingenuous. He asked the Israelites for a portion of the gold they had taken when plundering the Midianite army. He melted the gold, fashioned it into a special breastplate, and let the Israelites bow to it in superstitious worship.[18]

Gideon had seventy sons from his many wives. After Gideon's death, one of his sons, Abimelech, approached the men of his tribe and asked if it would not be better to be ruled by one man than by seventy. They liked the idea and gave him money to hire mercenaries to capture and kill all his brothers. Jotham, the only brother to escape this bloodbath, cursed Abimelech for wanting to be king and cursed those who supported his ambitions as well. Abimelech and his conspirators soon ended up destroying each other.[19]

As the years passed, the Israelites again turned from the LORD to worship Canaanite gods. By doing so, they became vulnerable to attacks by the Ammonites. After eighteen years of oppression, the Israelites cried out to God in their distress and were sent this message: "I saved your ancestors from all their enemies and yet you have turned to other gods. Let your new gods deliver you!" The Israelites recognized their foolishness and destroyed the idols and images of other gods.[20]

The next leader was Jephthah, the illegitimate son of a prostitute and Gilead, a tribal ruler. When Gilead's other sons were grown, they told Jephthah to leave because they did not want him to receive any inheritance. Everything changed when the Ammonite army came and attacked them. The Israelites could think of no one to lead them except the one they had disowned.[21]

Jephthah pointed out their hypocrisy, but agreed to lead them anyway, and sent messengers to ask the Ammonites why they were attacking. The Ammonites said they were only taking back what the Israelites had taken from them. Jephthah responded that

---

[18] Judges 8:24-27

[19] Judges 9:1-57

[20] Judges 10:6-14

[21] Judges 11:1-4

it had never been the Israelites' intention to do so, but when they had asked simply to pass through the lands in question, the Ammonites attacked them. More importantly, why had the Ammonites waited several generations to press their claim?[22]

| 4 | The Ammonite king rejected Jephthah's attempts at mediation, and prepared to attack. Jephthah wanted reassurance that God would be on his side, and vowed that if God granted him victory, he would sacrifice as a burnt offering whatever he first saw upon his return home. Jephthah triumphed over the Ammonites and came home to a celebration. To his dismay, the first thing he saw was his only child, a beautiful daughter, dancing with her tambourine in celebration of her father's victory. Fearing God's anger if he were to break his vow, Jephthah did what he had promised.[23]

Some Israelites threatened war because Jephthah had not given them a share of what he took from the Ammonites. Jephthah captured a river crossing and asked everyone to say 'Shibboleth.' Those who pronounced it 'Sibboleth' were put to death because their dialect proved they were from the tribe of Ephraim.[24]

The Israelites had gradually lost any sense that they were God's chosen people. Each tribe had lived in its own area for so long that they barely even spoke the same language. When enemies attacked, tribes responded on their own rather than banding together. The judges who followed Jephthah failed to deliver the Israelites from their enemies, but somehow managed to become rich in the process anyway.[25]

The Israelites had suffered for forty years under the Philistines when God raised up a man who would be neither a spiritual nor a military leader, but someone who would simply punish their enemies. An angel of the LORD came to an older, childless woman and told her she would finally have a son who was never

---

[22] Judges 11:5-24

[23] Judges 11:28-39

[24] Judges 12:1-6

[25] Judges 12:8-15

to have his hair cut because he would be a Nazirite, dedicated to God from birth. Even though the couple was excited at the idea of having a son, they prayed to God for help because they had no idea how to raise such a child.[26]

When their son, Samson, grew to be a man, he told his parents that he had found a Philistine that he wanted to marry. His parents were distressed that Samson would marry one of their enemies, but gave him what he wanted anyway.[27]

| 5 |

On the way to arrange the marriage, Samson killed a young lion. When he returned much later for the wedding, Samson enjoyed some honey he found in the lion's carcass. As the wedding feast began, Samson taunted the Philistines with a riddle: "Out of the eater, something to eat; out of the strong, something sweet." He said if the wedding party could answer his riddle, he would give new clothes to all of them, but if they failed to solve the riddle, they must give him new clothes.[28]

After three days of struggling with the riddle, they decided they could only win by cheating. They threatened to kill Samson's new wife and her family unless she told them what the riddle meant. Every day she begged Samson to tell her the answer as proof of his love for her, but he refused. On the last day of the wedding feast, Samson was finally worn down by her tears and told her the answer. She immediately passed the answer along and the wedding party said they had solved his riddle. Samson paid off the bet by killing thirty Philistines and giving their clothes to those who "solved" the riddle. Then Samson returned to his home, leaving his new wife behind.[29]

After some time had passed and Samson had cooled off, he went back to visit his wife, only to be told that she had been given to another man because her father thought Samson hated her. Infuriated again, Samson set fire to the grain fields, vineyards

---

[26] Judges 13:1-23

[27] Leviticus 5:2; 11:8-35; Judges 14:1-4

[28] Judges 14:10-14

[29] Judges 14:15-19

and olive groves of the Philistines. When they learned what had happened, the Philistines killed Samson's wife and her father.[30]

6 The cycle of violence and vengeance continued. Samson's enemies could think of no way to overcome his incredible strength until he gave them an opportunity by falling in love with Delilah, another Philistine. They offered her a huge reward if she could discover the secret of his strength. Three times Samson teased her with false answers and she complained that he was making her look like a fool. She kept after him, however, and eventually wore him down with her whining.[31]

Samson told Delilah that the real secret of his strength was his Nazirite vow never to cut his hair. The next time Samson fell asleep, Delilah shaved his head. When the Philistines attacked, he expected to defeat them as before, but the Spirit of God had left him. The Philistines overpowered Samson, gouged out his eyes and made him a slave.[32]

Eventually the Philistines held a great celebration to thank their god, Dagon, for delivering Samson into their hands. When they brought Samson out to taunt him, he placed his hands on the pillars of their temple and prayed for his strength to return for one final act of vengeance. The temple collapsed, killing Samson and everyone inside.[33]

The disintegration of the Israelites during 200 years of living in the Land had come to the point where they no longer paid attention to the Torah, but simply did whatever seemed right in their own eyes.

For instance, an Israelite from the tribe of Ephraim, stole a large amount of silver from his mother. When he heard his mother pronouncing curses on whoever had stolen it, he decided he had better give it back. She blessed him for his change of heart and

---

[30] Judges 15:1-6

[31] Judges 15:7 – 16:16

[32] Judges 16:17-21

[33] Judges 16:22-30

gave him the silver to make into an idol. The man was delighted to do so, and later found a Levite willing to serve as priest for the idol. When the tribe of Dan gathered an army to expand their territory, they decided to adopt this priest and idol as their own. Following a victorious campaign, the Danites set up a worship center for the idol.[34]

Another Levite living among the tribe of Ephraim had a mistress who was unhappy and unfaithful to him. When she went back to her home in Bethlehem, he pursued her and convinced her to return with him. On the journey home, they stopped in Gibeah, a town of the tribe of Benjamin. It looked like they might have to spend the night in the town square until a man welcomed them as guests in his home. Other men from the city came to the house and demanded that the visiting Levite come out and have sex with them. The owner of the house was shocked at such an idea and tried to send them away. When the men would not leave, the Levite sent his mistress out to them. They raped and abused her all night long and left her to die on the doorstep. The Levite took the body of his mistress and continued on his journey. When he returned home, he cut her body into twelve pieces and sent one to each of the tribes of the Israelites.[35]

Everyone was incensed, saying nothing like this had happened in all the years they had been in the Land. They decided to put to death the men of Gibeah who were guilty, but the tribe of Benjamin refused to hand them over. War followed and thousands were killed on both sides before the Benjaminites finally surrendered. Not only was the town of Gibeah destroyed, but all the other towns of Benjamin were destroyed as well. Nothing remained of Benjamin's tribe except 600 soldiers who had escaped to the desert.[36]

The Israelites regretted that their vengeance might have put an end to one of Israel's tribes. They saw no way to help, because in

---

[34] Joshua 19:40-47; Judges 17:1-13; 18:1-31

[35] Judges 19:1-29

[36] Judges 20:1-48

the midst of the war, they had made a vow to give no daughter in marriage to any Benjaminite. Rather than renounce their vow, they found a solution by remembering another vow they had taken: anyone who failed to go to war against the Benjaminites was to be destroyed. With misguided zeal and tortured logic, they attacked Jabesh Gilead, killing everyone except 400 virgins who were then given to the Benjaminites.[37]

7 Concerned that some men of Benjamin still lacked wives, the Israelites came up with a solution that was even more bizarre. They encouraged the men to kidnap unmarried women at a feast in Shiloh because in that way the fathers would not be guilty of breaking their vow: a father whose daughter was kidnapped could not be accused of having given his daughter in marriage.[38]

Even in the midst of such immorality, some sought to remain faithful to God. One such man left with his wife, Naomi, and their two sons during a famine to settle in Moab. The man died there and sometime later his sons died as well. Having decided to return to her homeland, Naomi bid farewell to her daughters-in-law. One of them, Ruth, insisted on going with her, saying, "Your people will be my people and your God my God."[39]

8 Naomi and Ruth traveled to Bethlehem, where Ruth supported them by gleaning grain from fields owned by Boaz, whose custom was to assist the poor this way in accordance with the Torah. Boaz fell in love with Ruth and married her, not only for her beauty, but for her devotion to her mother-in-law and her commitment to the LORD.[40]

Another faithful person during this time was Hannah, a childless woman who asked God to give her a son. When her prayer was answered and Samuel was born, she dedicated him to God for

---

[37] Judges 21:1-14
[38] Judges 21:15-23
[39] Ruth 1:1-18
[40] Leviticus 23:22; Ruth 1:19 – Ruth 4:13

lifelong service and sent him to live with Eli, the priest.[41]

Eli's own sons grew up to be corrupt priests who mocked God by caring only about themselves. When burnt sacrifices were offered, Eli's sons took the best parts for their own use rather than burning them on the altar as required. They were also promiscuous with the women who served at the Tabernacle, and paid no attention to any rebuke their father gave them.[42]

Even as Eli's sons were incurring God's wrath, Samuel was finding God's favor. In the middle of the night, Samuel heard God calling his name, but thought it was Eli calling him. Eli finally figured out what was happening and told Samuel to say, "Speak, LORD, for your servant is listening." God told him that Eli's sons were to be judged for the contemptible things they were doing, and Eli for his unwillingness to stop them. Samuel soon became known as God's prophet.[43]

Some time later, the Israelites were attacked by the Philistines and suffered great loss. They wondered what went wrong and decided the Ark of the Covenant should be brought into battle to guarantee God's assistance. The Philistines were terrified by the idea that the God of Israel would be fighting against them, but instead of discouraging them, it made them determined to fight that much harder. The Israelites were soundly defeated. Eli's sons died in the battle, and the Ark of the Covenant was captured by the Philistines and placed in the temple of Dagon, their god. When news of these disasters reached Eli, he fell off his chair and broke his neck.[44]

The Philistines didn't celebrate their victory for long. First, they found their statue of Dagon lying on the ground in front of the Ark of the Covenant. They replaced it, but found it on the ground again the next day, broken in pieces. Then a plague of tumors affected everyone in the town where the Ark was being kept. The

---

[41] 1 Samuel 1:1-28

[42] 1 Samuel 2:11-25

[43] 1 Samuel 3:1-21

[44] 1 Samuel 4:1-22; 5:1-2

Philistines moved the Ark from town to town, but the plague of tumors followed wherever it went.[45]

The Philistines realized they had made a serious mistake in taking the Ark and decided to return it. They put it on a cart pulled by two oxen and watched as the driverless cart headed straight into Israelite territory. Seventy people in the town where the Ark came to rest died when they tried to look inside it. The Ark was moved to another town to see if any calamity would follow, and none did.[46]

After recovering from their disaster with the Ark, the Philistines attacked again and the Israelites began to see the error of their ways. They asked Samuel to intercede with God on their behalf, and Samuel said if they were serious about returning to God, they would need to destroy all their idols and worship the LORD alone. The Israelites came together and confessed their sin.[47]

When the Philistines heard that the Israelites had gathered in one place, they decided it was a good time to attack them. The Israelites trembled in fear when they saw the enemy coming, but Samuel encouraged the people to have faith that God would be with them. Suddenly, loud thunder erupted and the Philistines began to panic. The Israelites seized the opportunity and chased them out of the country.[48]

To celebrate God's deliverance, Samuel built a stone monument and called it Ebenezer: "Thus far has the LORD helped us."[49]

When Samuel grew old, he appointed his sons to follow him, but his sons were corrupt, accepting bribes and perverting justice as they pleased. The people complained and said the tradition of being led by judges was inadequate. "Give us a king to lead us

---

[45] 1 Samuel 5:3-12

[46] 1 Samuel 6:1-21

[47] 1 Samuel 7:1-6

[48] 1 Samuel 7:7-11

[49] 1 Samuel 7:12-15

like all other nations," the people said.[50]

When Samuel turned to God for guidance, he was told, "It is not you they have rejected as leader, but me. They have rejected my leadership and rebelled against me from the time I brought them out of Egypt." God told Samuel to give the people a clear warning of what being ruled by a king would mean.[51]

Samuel spoke to the people and told them what a king would do:

- He will take your sons to fight his wars for him;

- He will take your sons to plant his fields and harvest his crops;

- He will take your daughters to be perfumers, cooks and bakers;

- He will take the best of your crops to feed the bureaucrats who work for him; and,

- He will take your money for his own use and make you feel you are slaves once again.[52]

The people considered these warnings, but persisted in their demand for a king to rule over them. Finally, God told Samuel, "Listen to the people and give them a king."[53]

---

[50] 1 Samuel 8:1-5
[51] 1 Samuel 8:6-9
[52] 1 Samuel 8:10-18
[53] 1 Samuel 8:19-22

Questions for Reflection/Discussion

1. What lessons has your generation learned (or failed to learn) from the generation that came before you? What lessons do you hope to pass on to the next generation?

2. Ancient Israel, a male-dominated society, was open to a capable woman like Deborah being in a position of leadership. To what extent is society open to women leaders today?

3. Under what circumstances have you, like Gideon, looked for reassurance before moving ahead with something difficult?

4. It is hard to imagine that Jephthah would choose to sacrifice his child rather than acknowledge the rashness of his vow. Can you think of a more recent example of a leader's pride resulting in dire consequences for others?

5. Samson's parents thought he was foolish to marry one of their enemies, but they et him do it anyway. What would you do if you had a grown child intent on doing something you believed was wrong?

6. Samson was incredibly naïve to trust Delilah with the secret of his strength. In what situations might it be foolish to trust someone today?

7. These tragic examples of rape and murder demonstrate that women had few rights in ancient times. Are women still being denied basic rights today? What are some examples?

8. Had it not been for famine and personal tragedy, Ruth and Boaz would never have met and become the great-grandparents of David, and ultimately ancestors of Jesus. What personal or world events coincided to bring your parents together?

CHAPTER 7:
SAUL AND DAVID

Having a king meant that one tribe of the Israelites would have more power than others because it would establish a dynasty. This would be quite a change because the judges who had ruled the Israelites on and off for more than two centuries had come from different tribes: Judah, Benjamin, Ephraim, Manasseh, Isacchar, Gilead and Dan.[1]

That God would single out the tribe of Benjamin for such an honor was a surprise to many. Although Saul was an impressive young man who stood head and shoulders above other Israelites, he expressed his doubts when told he was God's choice. After all, the tribe of Benjamin was the smallest because only 600 men had survived the civil war that followed the rape and abuse of the Levite's mistress.[2]

Samuel assured Saul that God had clearly revealed who was to be king. After honoring Saul with a feast and anointing him with oil, Samuel told Saul to go and meet several prophets who were giving ecstatic messages as they played musical instruments. If Saul would go to them, the Spirit of God would come upon him and he would be a changed man.[3]

Everything happened as Samuel had said, but Saul was still uncertain, saying nothing to his family about having been anointed king. When Samuel gathered the tribes of Israel to introduce the new king, Saul was hiding among the baggage. He finally came out to shouts of "Long live the king!"[4]

Saul didn't begin his rule as king by exercising royal power or

---

[1] Othniel was from the tribe of Judah; Ehud from Benjamin; Deborah from Ephraim; Gideon from Manasseh; Tola from Isacchar; Jephthah from Gilead; Samson from Dan; and Samuel from Ephraim

[2] 1 Samuel 9:1-21

[3] 1 Samuel 9:22 – 10:6

[4] 1 Samuel 10:7-24

living in splendor, but by going home to work in his fields. One day a messenger came to tell Saul that the Ammonites were accosting the tribe of Gilead. Saul's wrath was stirred and the Spirit of God came upon him. He assembled an army from all the tribes and soundly defeated the Ammonites. The Israelites held a great celebration to reaffirm Saul's kingship.[5]

As the end of Samuel's life drew near, he assembled the people to remind them that their heritage was one of both blessings and curses. He recounted how God had brought them out of Egypt and into the Promised Land, and how often they had rebelled and broken the covenant they had made with the LORD. He emphasized that their demand for a king was wrong-headed because it meant they were rejecting God as their rightful king. Then he went on to say all would still turn out well if only the people and the king followed God faithfully in accordance with the Torah.[6]

1 Saul failed to heed Samuel's advice. The Israelites were under the control of the Philistines, who had forbidden them to have iron spears or swords. Although Saul's army had almost no weapons, he felt compelled to attack the Philistines. Wanting to be sure God was with the Israelites and having grown tired of waiting for Samuel, Saul offered burnt sacrifices on his own. When Samuel found out what had happened, he told Saul that such blatant disregard of the Torah meant his kingship would be taken from him and given to another.[7]

Another foolish act by Saul involved his son Jonathan, who left camp early one morning to see what was happening with the Philistine army. Believing that God had given him a sign that he would be victorious, Jonathan attacked an army outpost. He was indeed successful and soon the entire Philistine army was in retreat. Saul sent his men after them, vowing to execute anyone

---

[5] 1 Samuel 11:1-15

[6] 1 Samuel 12:1-25

[7] 1 Samuel 13:1-22

who ate anything before the Philistines had been destroyed.[8]

Jonathan and the army pursued the Philistines all day long, fighting skirmishes along the way. At one point, they came upon some honey in the woods and Jonathan grabbed some to eat as they marched. He found himself energized for battle, but the soldiers looked at him in alarm. When asked why, they told him of his father's vow to kill any who ate along the way.[9]

Jonathan could see what a foolish vow his father had made, for having something to eat would have energized the soldiers. Indeed, the soldiers were so hungry that when the battle finally ended, they killed several animals and ate them with the blood still in them, a clear violation of the Torah.[10]

The next time Saul wanted to attack the Philistines, he sought assurance from a priest that God would be on his side. When no answer came, Saul concluded that someone in the army had sinned and would have to die. Ignoring the fact that his men had eaten bloody meat in violation of the Torah, Saul concluded that Jonathan was to blame for having tasted the honey. Saul declared that Jonathan would have to be executed, but the army refused to let the king in his foolishness put to death his far more sensible son.[11]

Some time later, Samuel told Saul to attack and completely destroy a country that had mistreated the Israelites during their exodus from Egypt. Saul did as he was told and met with great success, but then decided to bring the king and all the best sheep and cattle home with him. When Samuel confronted him, Saul explained that he had brought all the best animals back to offer as a sacrifice to God. Samuel told Saul that God found delight in obedience, not in burnt offerings or sacrifices.[12]

---

[8] 1 Samuel 14:1-24
[9] 1 Samuel 14:25-28
[10] 1 Samuel 14:29-35
[11] 1 Samuel 14:36-45
[12] 1 Samuel 15:1-21

Because Saul had rejected God's word, God rejected Saul as king. When Saul was told this by Samuel, he confessed his sin and admitted he had let his armies take the plunder because he was afraid they would be angry with him otherwise. Samuel left Saul that day and never saw him again.[13]

Samuel was depressed about what Saul had done until God sent him to anoint a new king. Then Samuel became afraid, knowing Saul would have him executed for doing such a thing. God told Samuel the new king could be anointed quietly in the midst of a sacrificial feast. Samuel was to go to Bethlehem and find Jesse, the grandson of Ruth and Boaz.[14]

4 Samuel invited Jesse and all his sons to a feast. When the oldest son came forward, Samuel was sure this impressive young man must be God's choice, but God said, "I do not judge a man by his outward appearances, but by his heart." God's response was the same as each of Jesse's sons came forward. Finally, Samuel asked if there were no other sons. Jesse said the only one left was his youngest, David, who was out in the fields tending sheep. When David appeared, God confirmed that this was indeed the one to be anointed as the next king.[15]

Not much changed outwardly for David at that point even though God's Spirit came upon him in a powerful way. It was the same Spirit that had departed from Saul, who had been left an evil spirit to torment him. Saul's attendants thought that someone who played the harp might bring the king some peace. They asked who might do such a thing and learned that David played the harp and was a man of great courage. Saul invited David to play for him and was pleased by what he heard.[16]

Some time later, Saul and his army prepared for war against the Philistines. Each army was camped on a mountainside waiting to

---

[13] 1 Samuel 15:22-35

[14] 1 Samuel 16:1-3; Ruth 4:21-22

[15] 1 Samuel 16:4-13

[16] 1 Samuel 16:14-23

do battle in the valley between. The Philistines had a champion, Goliath, a giant of a man who came out each day and issued a challenge: "Let your best man fight me; whichever side loses will serve the other."[17]

Goliath repeated his challenge every day, but no one dared fight him. When David came to visit his brothers who were serving in Saul's army, he heard Goliath's challenge and asked, "Who is this that defies the army of the living God?"[18]

David went to Saul and offered to accept Goliath's challenge. Saul scoffed at the idea of a young shepherd fighting a giant, but David assured the king that God had delivered him from lions and bears who had attacked his sheep, and that this was simply one more enemy for God to defeat. Seeing no better option, Saul accepted David's offer and gave him his own armor to wear. David said he would prefer to fight Goliath in his own way.[19]

5

David took his shepherd's staff and picked up five smooth stones for his sling. When Goliath saw David coming, he was insulted: "Am I a dog that you send someone after me with a stick?" David replied, "You come at me with sword and spear, but I come at you in the name of the LORD Almighty whom you have defied!" David ran toward Goliath, putting a stone in his sling as he did so. After David released it, the stone hit Goliath in the forehead, knocking him out cold. David quickly took Goliath's sword, and cut off his head. When the Philistines saw that their champion was dead, they turned and ran, giving the Israelites a great victory.[20]

Saul's delight in what David had done soon turned to jealousy and anger as he heard the crowds shout, "Saul has slain his thousands and David his tens of thousands." He began to look

---

[17] 1 Samuel 17:1-10
[18] 1 Samuel 17:11-26
[19] 1 Samuel 17:27-39
[20] 1 Samuel 17:40-51

for an opportunity to kill David, going so far as to throw a spear at him while David was playing his harp. When that failed, Saul sent David repeatedly into battle against the Philistines in the hope that they would kill him. He gave his daughter, Michal, to David in marriage, intending to guarantee David's loyalty even while creating personal problems for him.[21]

In spite of Saul's plans to kill him, David was thriving because of his faith and because of the love and loyalty he inspired. For instance, when David found himself and his men besieged by the Philistines, he said how wonderful it would be to have a cool drink of water from Bethlehem's well. That very night, three of his elite warriors broke through the Philistine lines, drew water from the well, and brought it back to him. David poured the water on the ground as an offering to God, saying he was not worthy to drink the water that had become so valuable by the sacrifice required to obtain it. The men were impressed.[22]

Even Saul's son and heir to the throne, Jonathan, loved David and wanted only to help him. Much to Saul's disgust, Jonathan protected David again and again. Saul's threats and violent outbursts continued until David became convinced he had no alternative but to leave the country.[23]

As he was leaving, David stopped to see a priest to ask for help. The priest gave him what he could and blessed him. From there David went to another country where he pretended to be insane in order not to be perceived as a threat to anyone. Next he returned to his homeland and lived in a desert cave. Others who were outcasts came to stay with him and soon he had about 400 men at his side.[24]

When Saul heard that David had returned, he set out with an army to kill him. Saul ordered the execution of the priest who

---

[21] 1 Samuel 18:1-29

[22] 2 Samuel 23:13-17; 1 Chronicles 11:15-19

[23] 1 Samuel 19:1 – 20:42

[24] 1 Samuel 21:1 –22:2; 1 Chronicles 12:1-22; Psalm 34; 56

had helped David earlier, but Saul's soldiers refused to carry out his orders. In frustration and rage, Saul turned to a foreign mercenary who killed 85 priests who had not betrayed David to Saul when they had the chance. When David heard what had happened, he felt responsible for causing the death of so many innocent men.[25]

David and his band of outcasts kept moving from place to place as Saul pursued him. At one point, Saul went into a cave to relieve himself, not knowing that it was the very cave where David was hiding. David's men whispered to each other that God had delivered their enemy into their hands, but David simply crept forward, cut off a corner of Saul's robe, and went back to the recesses of the cave.[26]

When Saul had returned to his army, David left the cave, approached them, and asked why Saul believed David to be his enemy. Had David not proven his loyalty by sparing Saul's life? Couldn't he have cut off Saul's life as easily as he cut off a corner of his robe?[27]

As he heard David's words, Saul felt remorse for his murderous intent. He could now see that David was a better man than he and would certainly rule as king one day. Saul admitted all this to David, asking only that Saul's family be spared when David came into power. David promised Saul it would be so.[28]

David and his men moved to another place in the wilderness, not far from where Nabal kept thousands of sheep and goats. David sent messengers to Nabal to see if he could spare any food for them. Nabal sent word back that, as far as he knew, David was only another outlaw on the run who deserved nothing and would receive nothing. David told his men to arm themselves because

[25] 1 Samuel 22:6-23; Psalm 52

[26] 1 Samuel 23:1 –24:7; Psalm 54; 57; 63

[27] 1 Samuel 24:8-15

[28] 1 Samuel 24:16-22

they would take vengeance on this arrogant and wealthy man.[29]

Nabal's beautiful and wise wife, Abigail, heard from the servants how rudely her husband had treated David's men. She instructed her servants to load up many donkeys with supplies and take them to David on her husband's behalf, but without his awareness. Abigail went to David as well, begging him to overlook her husband's arrogance and spare his life. Impressed by her words and the generosity of her spirit, David agreed.[30]

When Abigail returned home and told her husband what she had done, he had a heart attack and died. David heard of this and asked Abigail to marry him. She became his third wife, along with Saul's daughter, Michal, and Ahinoam, a woman David had married during his years of exile.[31]

It was not long before Saul once again became obsessed with finding David and killing him. As David saw the king's army camped in the valley, he asked one of his men to go with him on a raid. Late that night they crept into Saul's camp until they came to the place where Saul was sleeping, supposedly under the watchful eye of Abner, leader of his army. David's companion wanted to kill Saul, but David said it would not be right to take the life of God's anointed no matter how evil or deranged he had become. Instead, David took the king's spear and water jug with him and left the camp.[32]

From a distance, David began shouting and the camp awoke. He called out to Abner, shaming him for the poor way in which he had guarded the king. The stolen water jug and spear were proof that David could have killed Saul if he had wanted. When Saul heard that David had once again spared his life, he apologized

---

[29] 1 Samuel 25:1-13

[30] 1 Samuel 25:14-35

[31] 1 Samuel 25:36-44

[32] 1 Samuel 26:1-12

for what he had done and returned home with his army.[33]

David decided it was best to leave the country again because of Saul's repeated attempts to kill him. He lived among the Philistines, earning their trust by telling their king that all his raids were done in vengeance against the Israelites. David made sure that no one from the Philistine cities he attacked lived to tell otherwise.[34]

When the Philistines went to war against the Israelites, David was invited to join them. Saul trembled at the sight of the Philistine army and wanted reassurance from God before the battle began. Because Samuel had died and there was no other prophet who could give Saul any answers, he turned to a witch instead. Through her dark arts, she consulted the spirit of Samuel as Saul had requested.[35]

Samuel's message, brought by the witch, provided no comfort at all. Saul was told he had received no answer from God because God had rejected him completely. Saul and his sons would soon die in a battle won by the Philistines. When Saul heard the message, he collapsed in exhaustion and despair.[36]

Before the battle began, the commanders of the Philistine army approached their king and demanded that David and his men be sent home. They were concerned that David would turn against them in the midst of the battle and side with the Israelites.[37]

This turn of events was fortuitous because it allowed David to discover that his town had been attacked by raiders in his absence. The families of David and his followers had not been killed, but had been carried off to become slaves. David's men blamed him for what had happened, but he convinced them to go

---

[33] 1 Samuel 26:13-25

[34] 1 Samuel 27:1-12; 1 Chronicles 12:1-7

[35] 1 Samuel 28:1-15

[36] 1 Samuel 28:16-25

[37] 1 Samuel 29:1-11

with him to bring their families back.[38]

The pursuit continued until David and his men came to a major ravine where 200 stayed behind because they were too exhausted to cross. David and the remainder, with the assistance of an escaped slave, found the raiders, rescued the families, and ended up with great amounts of plunder.[39]

As David and his men returned, many of them argued that those who stayed behind should have their families returned to them, but should have no share of the plunder. David overruled them, arguing that it was God who had given them the victory and that everyone in the community should share in the success.[40]

While David and his men were involved with the rescue of their families, the battle between the Philistines and the Israelites went forward. Saul and most of his sons were killed as Samuel, through the medium, had predicted. David, grieving the tragic end that had come to Saul and Jonathan, composed a song in their honor. David settled in Hebron, where the tribe of Judah made him their king.[41]

David, however, was not the only king among the Israelites. Abner, the commander of Saul's army, had survived the battle with the Philistines. He took Ishbosheth, one of the remaining sons of Saul and proclaimed him king. Civil war followed as the house of David and the house of Saul fought each other. As the war raged on, David's side grew stronger and Saul's weaker.[42]

One day Abner decided he was being treated poorly by those he served after being criticized for sleeping with one of Saul's mistresses. He sent a message to David that he would help him become king of all the Israelites if they could negotiate a

---

[38] 1 Samuel 30:1-8

[39] 1 Samuel 30:9-20

[40] 1 Samuel 30:21-25

[41] 1 Samuel 31:1-13; 2 Samuel 1:1 – 2:7; 1 Chronicles 10:1-14

[42] 2 Samuel 2:8 – 3:1

settlement. David responded that he would, but only if Michal, the daughter Saul had given him in marriage years before, was returned to him.[43]

David's family had grown significantly by this time. Even though he now had six wives and a son from each – plus other children from several concubines – he insisted on his first wife being returned to him anyway. Consenting to David's demand, Abner took Michal from her current husband, who followed behind throughout the journey, weeping all the way.[44]

Abner's meeting with David produced an agreement that would end the war and make David king of all the Israelites. While David was negotiating this agreement, the leader of his own army, Joab, was absent. When Joab returned, he was furious that David had trusted Abner. Joab pursued Abner and killed him to settle a blood feud. This rash act threatened to restart the war.[45]

When David learned what Joab had done, he was distraught. He ordered an elaborate funeral that would honor the memory of Abner, and he forced Joab and his men to march at the head of the funeral procession. David wept aloud at Abner's tomb and composed a song to commemorate his valor. In this way, David convinced the Israelites that he had not brought about Abner's death, and they moved forward with their plans to anoint him king of all the Israelites.[46]

Thinking they were helping David's cause, two men assassinated Ishbosheth, the son of Saul who had been David's rival. They cut off his head and brought it to David, thinking they would be rewarded for killing the king's enemy. Instead David condemned them for their cowardice and arrogance, and had them executed.[47]

---

[43] 2 Samuel 3:6-14

[44] 2 Samuel 3:2-5; 2 Samuel 3:13-15; 1 Chronicles 14:3-7

[45] 2 Samuel 3:22-27

[46] 2 Samuel 3:28-39

[47] 2 Samuel 4:1-12

David was thirty years old when he was anointed king over all the Israelites. At first he ruled from Hebron, but later captured Jerusalem and turned it into "the city of David." The king of Tyre sent David carpenters and stone masons along with many cedar logs to build a grand palace there. This was the beginning of the golden age of Israel.[48]

---

[48] 2 Samuel 5:1-12; 1 Chronicles 11:1-47; 1 Chronicles 12:23-40; 1 Chronicles 14:1-2

Questions for Reflection/Discussion

1. Saul offered burnt sacrifices to gain God's assistance in a battle he was about to fight. Under what circumstances might God take sides in a war?

2. The unintended consequence of Saul's command that his army not eat until the battle was over was that his men were robbed of energy that would have helped them fight. Do we still have well-intentioned school, business or political leaders who create policies and programs that end up doing more harm than good? What are some examples?

3. When Saul's army suffered defeat, he blamed Jonathan for having broken the king's decree rather than blaming his army for having broken God's commandment. Why do you think Saul saw things as he did in this matter? In what situations today do you think leaders tend to lose perspective?

4. God chose David to be king because God judges by the heart rather than by outward appearances. To what extent do we choose leaders in school, business, or government because of how impressive they look rather than because of their ability, character, and integrity?

5. When David fought Goliath, he found success using his own weapons rather than the superior ones he was offered by King Saul. What lesson might we learn from this?

CHAPTER 8:
DAVID AND HIS SONS

1 Having rid the land of the Philistines, David was at last ready to bring the Ark of the Covenant to Jerusalem. Moving it proved more difficult than David had imagined. In the midst of the journey, the oxen stumbled. Uzzah reached out to steady the Ark, and was immediately struck dead.[1]

Such a turn of events made David think the Ark might be too dangerous to bring to Jerusalem. He left it in the care of a man to see if any calamity would befall him, but for three months the Ark brought blessings to the man and his entire household.[2]

This convinced David it would be safe to bring the Ark into Jerusalem if he did so very carefully. David searched the Torah to discover the proper means for moving the Ark and then proceeded with caution, but also with great celebration. Burnt offerings were sacrificed along the way, trumpets played and people danced in front of the Ark as it moved along. David joined in the celebration as well, taking off his royal robes and dancing with unrestrained joy before God.[3]

Not everyone was pleased at this. Michal chastised her husband for his vulgar display in front of the slave girls. David replied angrily that his joyful dance was not to entertain the girls, but to celebrate what God had done. His relationship with Michal was never the same.[4]

David appointed priests and Levites to carry out worship in the Tabernacle as the Torah prescribed. The king's joy was such that he composed songs of praise and gave them to the worship leaders.[5]

---

[1] 2 Samuel 5:17 – 6:6; 1 Chronicles 13:1-11; 14:8-17
[2] 2 Samuel 6:8-12; 1 Chronicles 13:12-14
[3] Deuteronomy 10:8; 2 Samuel 6:12-15; 1 Chronicles 15:1-28
[4] 2 Samuel 6:16-23; 1 Chronicles 15:29
[5] 1 Chronicles 16:4-42

After David had been at peace with his enemies for some time, he told the prophet Nathan that it didn't seem right that the king should live in a grand palace while the Ark of the Covenant was housed in a tent. Nathan agreed that what David said made sense, and told him to do what he wanted because God obviously had blessed everything he did.[6]

That night Nathan received a message from God for David:

Why do you want to build a temple for me to live in? Since bringing my people out of Egypt, I have been content to move from place to place with them in the tent of my dwelling. Have I ever asked for more?[7]

The message went on to say that David's son would be the one to build a temple, and that God would establish David's dynasty as one that would last forever.[8]

Now that David had triumphed over his enemies and received assurances of an unending dynasty, he extended grace to others. He began by honoring Saul's only remaining son, a crippled man who thought of himself as being useless and worthless.[9]

Later, David honored some of his fallen enemies. The Gibeonites demanded to be given seven descendants of Saul to settle a blood feud. After the seven had been cruelly executed, their bodies were left to rot. Rizpah, mother of two who had been slain, stood guard over the exposed bodies for months, refusing to let the birds or wild animals attack them. When news of what Rizpah was doing came to David, he was moved to put an end to such a disgrace. He ordered that the bones of the seven, along with those of Saul and Jonathan, be treated with respect and buried with honor.[10]

David was convinced that his military victories and prosperity

---

[6] 2 Samuel 7:1-3; 1 Chronicles 17:1-2

[7] 2 Samuel 7:5-7; 1 Chronicles 17:3-6

[8] 2 Samuel 7:8-16; 1 Chronicles 17:7-14

[9] 2 Samuel 9:1-12

[10] 2 Samuel 21:1-14

were blessings of God given as a reward for his righteousness. Perhaps it was this arrogance and sense of entitlement that blinded him to some of his flaws that soon became apparent.[11]

One night, as David was getting some fresh air on the roof of his palace, he noticed a beautiful woman bathing below. He sent a servant to find out who she was and learned she was Bathsheba, the wife of Uriah, one of David's elite warriors. David sent for her and she dutifully came to him. He slept with her and sent her away. Later, she sent word to David that she was pregnant.[12]

Bathsheba's husband was away with the army on a lengthy campaign. David, who no longer fought alongside his men because they had decided his life was too valuable to be put at risk, sent a message to Joab, his general, asking that Uriah be sent home to bring a status report. After Uriah gave his report, David told him to go home and see his wife before returning to battle. Uriah left, but slept at the palace entrance instead.[13]

David asked Uriah the next day why he didn't go home and Uriah said it wouldn't be right for him to enjoy his wife while the rest of the army was in harm's way. David asked him to stay one more day in order to have a feast in his honor. David got Uriah drunk, hoping that he would finally go home to Bathsheba. But Uriah spent another night at the palace entrance.[14]

David decided that something more drastic must be done if his adultery was to be hidden. He sent Uriah back with a private message for the general: "Attack the enemy and put Uriah at the point where the fighting is the fiercest. Then pull the rest of the troops back leaving Uriah to be struck down and die."[15]

This time everything went as David had planned and Uriah died. After an appropriate period of mourning, David had Bathsheba

---

[11] 2 Samuel 22:21-25; Psalm 18

[12] 2 Samuel 11:1-5

[13] 2 Samuel 11:6-9; 2 Samuel 21:15-17

[14] 2 Samuel 11:10-13

[15] 2 Samuel 11:14-15

brought to the palace and she became his eighth wife.[16]

God sent the prophet Nathan to David with a message:

A rich man and a poor man lived in the same town. The rich man owned a lot of sheep and cattle, but the poor man had only one little lamb that he had bought and raised. The lamb became a pet for him and his children. He even let it eat from his plate and drink from his cup and sleep on his lap. The lamb was like one of his own children.

One day someone came to visit the rich man, but the rich man didn't want to kill any of his own sheep or cattle and serve it to the visitor. So he stole the poor man's little lamb and served it instead. [17]

David's anger rose, saying anyone who showed such arrogance should be put to death. Nathan said, "You are the man!" God's judgment was that adultery, deceit, and murder such as David committed would be repeated within David's own family.[18]

David confessed his sin and was told by Nathan that he would not die, but the son born to him would. As soon as Nathan left, Bathsheba's son became ill and David became distraught. For seven days, he refused to eat as he asked God to spare the child's life. When the child died, David's servants hesitated to tell him, fearing that he might do something desperate.[19]

Instead, David simply returned to his room after hearing the news, washed himself, put on fresh clothes and asked for something to eat. When his servants questioned him, David explained that he could seek God's mercy and grace for the child only while there was still hope. Once the child was gone, nothing

---

[16] 2 Samuel 11:16-27

[17] 2 Samuel 12:2-4 (CEV)

[18] 2 Samuel 12:5-12

[19] 2 Samuel 12:13-18; Psalm 51

more could be done.[20]

David comforted his wife Bathsheba, and they later had a second son, Solomon, who was loved by God in a special way. God revealed to David that it was Solomon who would be the next king, the one to build a temple as David wanted.[21]

As time went by, serious problems plagued David's family as Nathan had predicted. Amnon, David's son by his second wife, became infatuated with Tamar, David's daughter by his fourth. Amnon knew their relationship was forbidden by the Torah, but his desire could not be quenched. One of David's nephews came up with a plan by which Amnon could have what he wanted.[22]

Amnon pretended to be ill and asked David if Tamar could make a special dish and bring it to him herself. David passed along his son's request and Tamar complied. When she came to his bedroom, Amnon grabbed Tamar and forced himself upon her.[23]

5 No sooner had the rape ended than Amnon's desire turned to hatred and he ordered Tamar to get away from him. When she refused to leave, he called his servants and had her thrown out. Knowing there was no way to remove her disgrace, Tamar went to the house of her brother, Absalom, and remained there – a desolate woman all her life.[24]

When David heard what had happened, he was furious that his oldest son and presumptive heir to the throne would behave so badly. Absalom was outraged that his sister would be disgraced in this way and was determined to gain his revenge.[25]

Two years passed before Absalom found his opportunity. When the wool had been gathered from his sheep, Absalom sent an invitation for the family to come and celebrate with him. David

---

[20] 2 Samuel 12:19-23

[21] 2 Samuel 12:24-25; 1 Chronicles 22:7-10

[22] 2 Samuel 13:1-5

[23] 2 Samuel 13:6-14

[24] 2 Samuel 13:15-20

[25] 2 Samuel 13:21-22

deferred, saying it would be too much of a burden for Absalom to entertain the royal entourage. Absalom then asked David to send Amnon, the presumptive heir, in his place. David was uncertain about this, but finally decided to send all his sons.[26]

When the feast was at its peak, Absalom's men attacked and killed Amnon as they had been instructed. The rest of David's sons returned to him and mourned the death of their brother. Absalom fled to another country and stayed there three years. David longed to see him, but would not allow himself to do so.[27]

Joab, one of David's closest advisers, wanted the family to be reconciled. He arranged for a woman to approach the king and ask that the life of her son be spared. She said she was a widow whose only two sons had argued and one had taken the other's life because there had been no one to settle their dispute. Now the rest of her clan demanded the death of her remaining son, partly for the sake of justice, but also because they wanted her family's land. She asked David to intervene to prevent her from becoming a childless widow and he agreed to do so.[28]

The woman then asked the king why he was willing to show mercy to her son but not to his own? David began to see the truth of what she was saying, and also began to see the hand of Joab in all of this. He called for Joab and told him that Absalom could return to Jerusalem, but that he must remain outside the palace and not come into the king's presence.[29]

Now that Absalom was back in Jerusalem, he developed a plan to strengthen his position as David's oldest remaining son and presumptive heir to the throne. He allowed two years to pass without asking for anything. Then he called for Joab to come and speak to him. When Joab repeatedly ignored his request, Absalom burned Joab's fields to get his attention. Joab finally came, and Absalom insisted he gain an audience for him with the

---

[26] 2 Samuel 13:23-27

[27] 2 Samuel 13:28-39

[28] 2 Samuel 14:1-11

[29] 2 Samuel 14:12-24

king. Joab did so and David was reconciled to Absalom.[30]

| 6 | Absalom continued his plan by sitting regularly at the main gate to the city. As people approached, he asked their business. If they sought help from the king, he would tell them he could guarantee their success. When they tried to thank him for his assistance, he assured them that it was his pleasure to serve them. After four years of doing this, Absalom had won the hearts of the people.[31]

Absalom asked the king for permission to go to Hebron to fulfill a vow he had made to worship God in the city where David had been anointed king. David agreed, and Absalom took with him 200 men from Jerusalem. He also sent messengers throughout Israel telling them to shout "Absalom is king in Hebron" as soon as they heard the trumpets.[32]

David learned what was happening and realized he had lost control of the country. Fearing that Absalom might begin his reign with a murderous rampage, David gathered those who were loyal to him and fled the city, leaving only ten of his concubines to take care of the palace. The priests wanted go with David and take the Ark of the Covenant with them, but David told them to stay in Jerusalem.[33]

David's departure was met with mixed reactions. The crippled son of Saul shown kindness by David earlier returned the favor now by sending food and supplies for David's entourage. However, another descendant of Saul cursed and taunted David, saying David was getting what he deserved for all the blood he had shed. One of David's men wanted to silence him, but David said if his own son hated him, why should he expect better from his enemies?[34]

---

[30] 2 Samuel 14:25-33

[31] 2 Samuel 15:1-6

[32] 2 Samuel 15:7-12

[33] 2 Samuel 15:13-30; Psalm 3

[34] 2 Samuel 16:1-12

As Absalom entered Jerusalem, he sought advice from his counselors concerning what he should do to consolidate his grip on David's kingdom. His top adviser told him to sleep with the ten concubines David had left behind and let everyone know about it. Doing this would show that David was powerless and Absalom neither respected nor feared him.[35]

Absalom's top adviser encouraged him to take a small army that could travel quickly and pursue David and those

| 7 |

who had left with him. Another adviser, who was loyal to David, encouraged Absalom to show more caution in light of David's many military triumphs. It would be better to take the time to raise a huge army from the entire country in order to guarantee victory. Absalom was swayed by this argument.[36]

The extra time David was given allowed him to cross the Jordan River and organize his defenses. David divided his small army into three sections, each of which had outstanding leaders who knew how to use the wooded terrain to their advantage. Although David wanted to lead his men into battle, they insisted his life was worth more than 10,000 of theirs. David reluctantly stayed behind, telling his men to treat Absalom gently for his sake.[37]

Absalom's army – unused to the wooded terrain – was soundly defeated, and as Absalom was fleeing, his head became stuck in the branch of a tree. One of David's soldiers told Joab what had happened and Joab asked if he had killed Absalom. The soldier said he could never do such a thing after hearing David tell everyone to treat Absalom gently, but Joab saw things differently. Despising Absalom for the way he had treated David, Joab and his men went back to where Absalom was stuck in the tree and killed him on the spot.[38]

Joab sent a messenger to David with the good news: "The LORD

---

[35] 2 Samuel 16:15-22

[36] 2 Samuel 17:1-14

[37] 2 Samuel 17:15 – 18:5

[38] 2 Samuel 18:6-17

has delivered you from your enemies!" David was pleased by this, but was overcome with grief when told of his son's death, weeping loudly and saying repeatedly, "O Absalom, my son, my son! If only it had been I who died instead of you!"[39]

8   Joab was outraged when he heard of David's reaction to Absalom's death for he knew how his soldiers would respond. Indeed, they returned to David with heads held low, feeling shame for disappointing the king rather than feeling worthy of honor for having saved his life and kingdom. Joab confronted David and said the army would abandon the king unless he showed them some respect for having risked their lives. David forced himself to do what Joab told him was necessary.[40]

After Absalom's death, it was not a simple matter for David to return to the throne from which he had been deposed. He would either need to force his way back or wait until he was invited to return. David chose the latter, building on people's positive memories of the early years of his reign and negotiating new alliances throughout the country. David even let it be known that Amasa, the man who had led Absalom's army, would lead the army of all the Israelites if David became king again.[41]

David's plan worked and he was welcomed back to Jerusalem. Even those who had taunted and mocked him as he left came and begged David not to take revenge on them. Saying this was to be a time of gratitude rather than vengeance, David sought to be equitable in settling disputes that had arisen in his absence.[42]

Even with David's efforts, the country was badly divided. Sheba, a man from the tribe of Benjamin, denounced David and began a new rebellion, leading David to conclude that such a man could do more damage than even Absalom had done. David sent his army in pursuit, determined to stamp out the rebellion before

---

[39] 2 Samuel 18:18-33

[40] 2 Samuel 19:1-8

[41] 2 Samuel 19:9-15

[42] 2 Samuel 19:16-30

things got out of hand. Amasa went to take command of the army as David had promised, but Joab assassinated him, kept control of the army, and ended the rebellion.[43]

David had other disagreements with Joab. David decided to take a census because knowing how many able-bodied men were in the country would let him know how large an army he could draft and how many workers he could conscript for building projects. Joab and the army resisted because they knew how much trouble such a census could create, but David persisted.[44]

When the census was complete, David realized how arrogantly he had acted. He was not surprised when a prophet came to confront him with his sin, but he was unprepared when asked to choose his punishment: three years of famine, three months of war or three days of plague. David said his choice would be anything but war because he believed he was more likely to find mercy in the hands of God than in the hands of men.[45]

A plague soon swept across the land as the prophet had foretold and thousands died. Before the three days were up, however, God grieved for what was happening and put an end to the plague. David established an altar at the site where the plague stopped and worshipped God there. It was the very spot where the Temple would one day be built. He began accumulating the necessary materials for such a project even though he knew it would be Solomon who would be the one to build the Temple.[46]

As the end of David's life drew near, he became infirm and needed the assistance of a nurse. She would even sleep with him, though not for sex, but to keep him warm. David's oldest son, Adonijah, saw how infirm his father was and decided to take over the throne. Such willfulness was not surprising because Adonijah, who was handsome and charming, had received little

---

[43] 2 Samuel 20:1-13

[44] 2 Samuel 24:1-9; 1 Chronicles 21:1-7

[45] 2 Samuel 24:10-14; 1 Chronicles 21:8-13

[46] 2 Samuel 24:15-25; 1 Chronicles 21:14-30; 22:1-5

discipline from his father at any time in his life.[47]

With the support of several priests and military leaders, Adonijah made preparations to be declared king by inviting royal officials from his tribe to a great feast. The prophet Nathan was not invited, but learned of it anyway and sent word to Bathsheba that she must act quickly on behalf of Solomon.[48]

Bathsheba went to David and asked if he knew what Adonijah was doing. She reminded David of his promise that Solomon would be his successor and asked him to do something before it was too late. While she was speaking to David, Nathan came in and confirmed everything she said. David declared that Nathan and one of David's loyal priests would anoint Solomon as king that very day.[49]

David encouraged Solomon to be faithful to the Torah, and told his officials to work closely with Solomon in building the Temple in accordance with the plans David had been given by God. David said to use his wealth to build the Temple, and then encouraged everyone else to contribute to the project as well.[50]

Then David sang praises to God and prayed:

> *But who am I, and who are my people, that we could give anything to you? Everything we have has come from you, and we give you only what you first gave us! We are here for only a moment, visitors and strangers in the land as our ancestors were before us. Our days on earth are like a passing shadow, gone so soon without a trace.*

> *O LORD our God, even this material we have gathered to build a Temple to honor your holy name comes from you! It all belongs to you! I know, my God, that you examine our hearts and rejoice when you find integrity there. You know I have done all this with good motives, and I have*

---

[47] 1 Kings 1:1-6

[48] 1 Kings 1:7-12

[49] 1 King 1:13-39

[50] 1 Chronicles 22:11-19; 28:1-21; 29:1-9

watched your people offer their gifts willingly and joyously.

O LORD, the God of our ancestors Abraham, Isaac, and Israel, make your people always want to obey you. See to it that their love for you never changes. Give my son Solomon the wholehearted desire to obey all your commands, laws, and decrees, and to do everything necessary to build this Temple, for which I have made these preparations. [51]

Solomon's anointing as king was then celebrated by a great parade with many people marching, shouting and playing flutes. When Adonijah heard the celebration, he knew his attempt to be named king had failed. Adonijah asked Solomon for mercy and was told that he would receive it if he proved worthy of it.[52]

In his final words, David told Solomon that if he would only be faithful to the Torah, his reign would be long and prosperous and his descendants would reign forever. David then asked Solomon to take vengeance on those who had treated him badly during his life and show favor to those who had helped him.[53]

---

[51] 1 Chronicles 29:14-19 (NLT)

[52] 1 Kings 1:40-53

[53] 1 Kings 2:1-12

Questions for Reflection/Discussion

1. Uzzah was struck dead for touching the Ark when he thought it was going to fall off the ox cart. When things start to go wrong, are we more likely to react impulsively or be patient and trust that everything will be okay?

2. David's plan to build a temple made sense to Nathan, but it was not what God wanted. Are you ever tempted to think that what you want is what God wants? Give an example.

3. How many bad decisions (sinful choices) did David make in regard to Bathsheba and Uriah? What stories from our time show how easily one bad decision can follow another?

4. Was David's behavior regarding Bathsheba's child a model for us to follow or one for us to avoid? How do you think you would have acted?

5. Amnon's desire for his sister turned to hatred after he raped her. How are we to understand such a change of heart?

6. Absalom furthered his political ambitions by giving people whatever they wanted. How many politicians do you think put the interests of the country above their personal interests and the interests of their political party? Why do they do that?

7. Absalom was led astray by an adviser loyal to David. Have you ever been given advice by someone who did not have your best interests in mind? Give an example.

8. David's love for his rebellious son, Absalom, was extreme. Do you think it was a healthy love or an unhealthy one? In what ways is it similar to or different from God's love for us?

CHAPTER 9:
SOLOMON AND CIVIL WAR

After David had died, Adonijah, the son who had hoped to be king, asked for an audience with Bathsheba. He told her that he had accepted his fate, but asked her to make one request from Solomon: could the beautiful young nurse who had been taking care of David be given to Adonijah as his wife? Bathsheba took this request to Solomon, who promptly ordered Adonijah's death. Asking to marry the woman who had been sleeping with the king was proof enough to Solomon that Adonijah still had hopes of one day claiming the throne.[1]

Solomon then dealt with others who had been unfaithful to King David. The priest who sought to anoint Adonijah was not killed, but was banished from the priesthood. The army general who supported Adonijah was not so lucky; Solomon ordered his death in vengeance for the innocent blood he had shed. The descendant of Saul who had cursed and taunted David was told his life would be spared as long as he never left Jerusalem. Three years later the man left Jerusalem to pursue two slaves who had escaped from him. Solomon had him executed, noting that the man had determined his own fate.[2]

Having settled these internal problems, Solomon now sought to build external alliances. The first one set the pattern for many to follow: Solomon negotiated a treaty with Egypt's pharaoh and married his daughter to confirm the alliance. This was a clear violation of the Torah. An even clearer violation was Solomon's habit of worshipping God not solely at the Tabernacle, but at all the competing altars that had been established by people throughout the Land for various reasons over the years.[3]

In spite of Solomon's violations of the Torah, God appeared to him in a dream and asked what he wanted more than anything.

---

[1] 1 Kings 2:13-25
[2] 1 Kings 2:26-46
[3] 1 Kings 3:1-4

Solomon said he was overwhelmed by the responsibilities he faced as king and would ask only for the wisdom to know right from wrong when decisions had to be made. God was pleased that Solomon had asked for this rather than for long life, great wealth, worldwide fame or the death of his enemies. God told Solomon he would give him not only the wisdom he asked for, but everything else as well. Long life and peace would not be automatic, however, but would come if Solomon was faithful to the Torah. When Solomon awoke from his dream, he returned to Jerusalem and offered many sacrifices of thanksgiving at the Tabernacle.[4]

It was not long before Solomon's wisdom was put to the test by two prostitutes who lived with their infant sons in the same house. During the night, one woman's baby died. She crept into the other woman's bedroom and switched babies. When the mother woke up in the morning with the dead baby at her side, she knew she had been deceived, but the other woman denied it.[5]

The two women went to the king and asked him to settle their dispute. He heard their claims and announced the verdict: the living child should be cut in two and each woman given half. The deceitful mother agreed, but the true mother said she would rather give up her son than have him put to death. Solomon gave the child to the one who was willing to save the child's life. Word of his wise handling of this situation spread far and wide.[6]

Solomon's wisdom and learning were evident in many areas. In addition to composing countless songs and proverbs, he recorded details of plants, animals, birds and fish. He instituted a system of taxation that required each of the twelve areas of Israel to provide one month of supplies each year for the royal household. Such taxes were heavy, but people were willing to pay them to maintain peace and prosperity. Even Solomon's enemies sent

---

[4] 1 Kings 3:5-15; 2 Chronicles 1:7-12
[5] 1 Kings 3:16-22
[6] 1 Kings 3:23-28

large amounts of money to avoid war with him and his allies.[7]

Solomon was now ready to build the grand Temple that David had first envisioned. He began by agreeing to buy cedar logs at an exorbitant price from the famed forests of Lebanon. Then he drafted every able-bodied man to work for him, requiring that they spend one month in labor and two months at home. Some went to Lebanon to prepare the cedar logs while others worked in quarries to remove large blocks of stone.[8]

The central portion of the Temple was 90 feet long, 30 feet wide and 45 feet high, with additional storage rooms on both sides and a porch in front. Inside the Temple was a cubic room thirty feet on each side that would be the Holy of Holies. This inner room was overlaid with gold; the remainder of the interior was lined with cedar and had carvings of angels, trees and flowers. The Temple furnishings – a table, altar and lamp stands like those in the Tabernacle – were made of pure gold.[9]

In the midst of construction, Solomon received a message from God:

> *Concerning this Temple you are building, if you keep all my decrees and regulations and obey all my commands, I will fulfill through you the promise I made to your father, David. I will live among the Israelites and will never abandon my people Israel.*[10]

When construction on the Temple was finished, the Ark of the Covenant was brought from the Tabernacle and placed in the Temple. As this happened, the glory of the LORD filled the Temple as a cloud. Solomon offered a prayer of thanksgiving and dedication, recognizing that God could not be contained within any building, but that his Name could be there. Solomon went on to ask God to be attentive to those who prayed within

---

[7] 1 Kings 4:7-34; 2 Chronicles 9:13-28

[8] 1 Kings 5:1-18; 2 Chronicles 2:1-17; 8:7-10

[9] 1 Kings 6:1-10; 6:14-36; 7:13-51; 2 Chronicles 3:1-17; 4:1-22

[10] 1 Kings 6:12-13 (NLT)

the Temple and to those who from a distance prayed with the Temple in mind, forgiving all who acknowledged their sins and turned their hearts toward God.[11]

2 After Solomon finished his prayers of dedication, he challenged the Israelites to live fully in accordance with the Torah. Then he sacrificed vast quantities of cattle and sheep in thanksgiving and dedication, and all the people celebrated with a great feast.[12]

That night, God appeared to Solomon in a dream with words of encouragement and warning. The Israelites should not assume they can live however they choose without consequences, but neither should they ever lose hope:

> *When I shut up the heavens so that there is no rain, or command locusts to devour the land or send a plague among my people, if my people, who are called by my name, will humble themselves and pray and seek my face and turn from their wicked ways, then will I hear from heaven and will forgive their sin and will heal their land.*[13]

God's message in the dream continued with assurances that Solomon's dynasty would be established forever if he would live and rule in accordance with the Torah. Worshipping other gods, however, would bring devastating consequences.[14]

It had taken seven years to complete the construction and consecration of the Temple. Over the next thirteen years, Solomon continued to use forced labor for building many palaces. His administrative palace alone was four times larger than the Temple. Other palaces included one for his living quarters and another for Pharaoh's daughter.[15]

As the years went by, Solomon's wealth and wisdom continued

---

[11] 1 Kings 8:1-54; 2 Chronicles 5:1-14; 6:1-42

[12] 1 Kings 8:55-66; 2 Chronicles 7:1-10

[13] 2 Chronicles 7:13-14 (TNIV)

[14] 1 Kings 9:1-9; 2 Chronicles 7:15-22

[15] 1 Kings 6:37-38; 1 Kings 7:1-12

to grow. The Queen of Sheba heard of this and came to test Solomon with hard questions. She was so impressed with his answers and with his incredible wealth that she said his reputation failed to do him justice. Others who came to visit Solomon were equally impressed by what they saw and heard.[16]

Unfortunately, this was not the nature of kingship intended by God. Moses had brought God's warning from the beginning that kings were not to build large armies, marry many wives, accumulate great wealth or consider themselves better than others or above the law.[17]

Solomon's most blatant transgression was marrying women from nations God had specifically told the Israelites to avoid. Ultimately he ended up with 700 wives and 300 concubines, many of whom led him into worship of false gods. Some of these religions were particularly detestable because their worship involved temple prostitution and human sacrifices.[18]

God's judgment on Solomon first took the shape of enemies rising against him. Even as the era of peace and prosperity was coming to an end, Solomon's dynasty was threatened as well. God sent a prophet to Jeroboam, the leader of Solomon's workforce. Tearing his cloak into twelve pieces, the prophet gave ten pieces to Jeroboam and said these represented the tribes of Israel that would be his to rule following Solomon's death. The prophet told Jeroboam that his kingdom would be blessed and sustained as long as he remained faithful to the LORD and did not chase after other gods.[19]

When Solomon died, his son, Rehoboam, became king. The people asked if he would lift the burden of taxation and forced labor they had experienced under Solomon's reign. The new king asked his father's advisers how he should respond, and they

---

[16] 1 Kings 10:1-13; 2 Chronicles 9:1-12
[17] Deuteronomy 17:14-20
[18] 1 Kings 11:1-13
[19] 1 Kings 11:14-39

told him there was no longer any need for the demands Solomon had made upon the people. Granting their request and easing their burden would win the hearts of the people.[20]

Rehoboam heard what his father's advisers had to say, and then consulted the young men who had long been his friends. They told him to do just the opposite: the new king should treat the people even more harshly in order to gain their fear and respect. The new king listened to his young friends and told the people of Israel that he was twice the man his father had been and they should expect their burdens to be doubled as well.[21]

4 When Jeroboam and others heard the new king's arrogant words, they told him he might be the leader of his tribe, but the other tribes had no reason to swear their allegiance to him. Since he cared nothing about them, they would care nothing about him. The people of ten tribes abandoned the new king and went back to their homes. Rehoboam sent the head of forced labor after the people to bring them back, but they stoned him to death instead. Rehoboam realized he had lost his kingdom.[22]

The ten tribes of Israel who abandoned Rehoboam decided it would be good to come together as one with Jeroboam as their king. Rehoboam, now the king of Judah, gathered an army from his tribe and from the tribe of Benjamin. He was ready to go to war against Jeroboam until a prophet came to him and said attacking his brothers would be a grave mistake because the division of the kingdom could not be undone. Rehoboam listened to the prophet and returned to his father's palace in Jerusalem. Then he fortified the cities of Judah and Benjamin for the conflict he was sure would come.[23]

King Jeroboam of Israel established Shechem as the capital city of the northern tribes. He soon saw a problem: the people who supported him would be tempted to give their allegiance to King

---

[20] 1 Kings 12:1-7; 2 Chronicles 10:1-7

[21] 1 Kings 12:8-15; 2 Chronicles 10:8-15

[22] 1 Kings 12:16-18; 2 Chronicles 10:16-19

[23] 1 Kings 12:20-24; 2 Chronicles 11:1-12

Rehoboam of Judah if they regularly went to Jerusalem to worship at the Temple. In order to avoid this, Jeroboam had two golden calves made. He placed them in the cities of Dan and Bethel, saying to the people, "These are the gods who brought your ancestors out of Egypt and into this land." The king also appointed his own priests for these shrines and declared new festivals to be celebrated. Jeroboam told his people that these new worship centers eliminated any need for them to go to Jerusalem.[24]

The problem with all this, of course, is that it was a direct violation of the Torah, voiding God's promise that Jeroboam would have peace, prosperity and a long reign. A prophet from Judah came to Jeroboam, who was offering sacrifices at the shrine in Bethel. The prophet told the king that a descendant of David would one day destroy the shrine and sacrifice the false priests on its altar.[25]

Jeroboam stretched out his hand and ordered the prophet to be seized, but as the king did so, his hand shriveled up. Jeroboam asked the prophet to intercede with God for his hand to be healed. The prophet did so and the king showed his gratitude by inviting the prophet to dinner. The man refused, saying his message from God was to eat and drink nothing on the journey.[26]

As the prophet was returning to Judah, a prophet from **5** Bethel followed after him. When the two met, the prophet from Bethel lied to the other prophet, saying he had received a message from God that the prophet should come to his home. The prophet from Judah accepted this word, bringing judgment on himself. When he resumed his journey, a mountain lion attacked and killed him.[27]

King Jeroboam, having learned nothing from his encounter with the prophet, continued to appoint unqualified priests to maintain

---

[24] 1 Kings 12:25-33

[25] 1 Kings 13:1-2

[26] 1 Kings 13:4-10

[27] 1 Kings 13:11-32

the false worship sites. When his son became ill and nothing could be done for him, the king sent his wife in disguise to an old prophet. Though the prophet was blind and could not have recognized the king's wife anyway, God told the prophet who she was even before she spoke to him.[28]

The message given the king's wife by the prophet was a devastating one. He said the kingdom would be torn away from Jeroboam because of the false worship he had established. The son who was ill would die, but he would be the fortunate one because all the other sons of the king would suffer cruel and horrible deaths and not even be buried with honor. The ten tribes of Israel would suffer as well because of their complicity in this false worship. The day would come when they would be overrun by an enemy and carried away to distant lands.[29]

Things were going no better back in Judah. King Rehoboam, having learned nothing from his disastrous decision that split the country, established false worship centers throughout Judah's territory. They followed the worship practices of those who had been driven out of the land by Joshua, even to the extent of having male temple prostitutes.[30]

6 Tensions and rivalries between Judah and Israel eventually led to war, and as the war continued, both kingdoms became weak and vulnerable. God's judgment on Judah came when the king of Egypt attacked Jerusalem and carried off gold treasures from the Temple and from Solomon's palaces. God told Rehoboam that he would not be destroyed, but he would be forced to serve the king of Egypt to learn the difference between serving God and man.[31]

Judah suffered through twenty years of leadership by Rehoboam and his son until Asa became king. Though his father had been unfaithful to the LORD, Asa was different from the beginning.

---

[28] 1 Kings 13:33-34; 1 Kings 14:1-6

[29] 1 Kings 14:7-18

[30] 1 Kings 14:21-24; 2 Chronicles 11:13-23

[31] 1 Kings 14:25-28; 2 Chronicles 12:2-15

He reigned for forty years, reaffirming the Torah and replacing many of the Temple and palace treasures. He also expelled male shrine prostitutes from the land and destroyed false idols that were being worshipped. King Asa even deposed his grandmother for having established a false worship center.[32]

Asa's long rule was characterized not only by religious reform, but by successfully resisting attacks by Jeroboam and the kings who followed him in Israel. For many years, Asa prevailed over all his enemies because he depended on God. Eventually, though, Asa decided to forge an alliance with the king of Damascus on the northern border of Israel. Such an alliance would make Israel vulnerable to attacks by Damascus from the north and Judah from the south. This made sense militarily, but the prophet Hanani told Asa it was a bad decision. Asa responded by having the prophet thrown in prison for daring to criticize the king.[33]

One of Jeroboam's sons succeeded him as king of Israel, but was assassinated shortly after his reign began. The man who seized control of the throne, Baasha, immediately put to death everyone in Jeroboam's family, thus fulfilling the dire prophecy given to Jeroboam's wife years before.[34]

The new king of Israel continued to support the false worship centers Jeroboam had established earlier at Dan and Bethel. Because of this, a prophet from God brought a message that the fate of King Baasha's family would be the same as that of Jeroboam. When Baasha's reign ended and his son assumed the throne, one of the king's officials, Zimri, assassinated the new king, killed the rest of the royal family, and claimed the throne for himself.[35]

Zimri's reign didn't last long. Within a matter of days he was attacked by enemies, and chose to take his own life by setting his

---

[32] 1 Kings 15:9-15; 2 Chronicles 14:1-8; 15:1-19

[33] 1 Kings 15:16-22; 2 Chronicles 13:1-22; 14:9-15; 16:1-14

[34] 1 Kings 15:25-30

[35] 1 Kings 15:33-34; 16:1-13

palace on fire. A struggle for leadership followed, and Omri, the commander of the army, emerged as the new king. He established Samaria as the capital city of Israel and ruled the ten tribes of the northern kingdom for twelve years before being succeeded by Ahab, his son.[36]

Jeroboam and his descendants had wreaked havoc in Israel for more than fifty years by their refusal to follow the Torah. Omri and his son, Ahab, would prove no better.

---

[36] 1 Kings 16:15-28

Questions for Reflection/Discussion

1. Solomon asked God to hear the prayer of those whose minds were focused on the Temple when they prayed. Where is your mind most often focused when you pray? Does your focus make a difference in how you experience prayer?

2. Solomon told people to follow the Torah even while he violated its commandment not to marry foreign wives or worship foreign gods. Do we still have political and religious leaders who fail to practice what they preach? Give some examples.

3. Solomon made some foolish decisions even though he had great wisdom. In what ways can intelligence and education make life more difficult? In what ways can they be helpful?

4. Rehoboam thought it would be better for a king to be feared than loved. Can you think of leaders in today's world who seek to be feared and others who seek to be loved? How about bosses? Is one type or the other more successful?

5. The prophet from Judah paid a price for trusting someone who intentionally deceived him. Are you more likely to be too skeptical or too trusting of others? What forces have shaped your thinking in this regard?

6. The war between Judah and Israel weakened both countries. Is this something that often happens in wars today? If wars are so devastating, why do they seem so unavoidable?

7. Hanani was thrown in prison for criticizing the king. Under what conditions would you confront someone in a position of authority? Would you ever risk prison for your principles?

CHAPTER 10:
AHAB AND JEZEBEL

King Ahab's reign descended to new lows regarding faithfulness to the Torah. He not only married Jezebel, the daughter of a foreign king, but he also built a temple for worship of Baal in Samaria, and a totem pole for worship of Baal's consort, Asherah, "the goddess of fertility." This provoked the LORD's anger more than anything done by the kings who preceded him.[1]

| 1 | The prophet Elijah came to King Ahab with a warning from God. Because Ahab worshipped Baal, the false god of rain, there would be no rain in Israel until the prophet of the LORD gave the word.[2]

After giving Ahab his message, Elijah crossed the Jordan River as God told him and stayed near a small stream. God provided for Elijah in the desert by sending ravens to him with food. When the stream dried up from extended lack of rain, God sent Elijah to the homeland of Queen Jezebel, saying that a widow in that country would provide for him.[3]

Elijah came to the town gate, and found a woman gathering sticks. He asked for a drink of water and a small piece of bread if she could spare any. She replied that she would share with him what she had, but it would be their last meal. When her small amount of oil and flour were gone, she and her son would surely die. Elijah told her if she shared what she had with him, her supplies would last until the drought came to an end.[4]

Some time later, the widow's son became increasingly ill. When the boy stopped breathing, the widow became angry at Elijah, saying he had saved her son's life only to watch him die. Elijah took the lifeless boy and laid him on a bed. Three times Elijah lay on top of him and asked God to bring the child back to life.

---

[1] 1 Kings 16:29-33

[2] 1 Kings 17:1

[3] 1 Kings 17:2-9

[4] 1 Kings 17:10-16

God heard Elijah's prayer and the breath of life returned to him.[5]

After three years, the word of the LORD came to Elijah saying it was time to go back to King Ahab and put an end to the drought. As Elijah approached, the king said, "Here comes the trouble-maker." Elijah replied that it was Ahab who had brought trouble on the Israelites by rejecting the Torah and worshipping false gods. Elijah told King Ahab to summon the people to Mt. Carmel and to bring the 450 prophets of Baal and the 400 prophets of Asherah who were devoted to Queen Jezebel.[6]

When the people gathered, Elijah told them they could worship the LORD or they could worship Baal, but worshipping both was not an option. Elijah told the prophets of Baal to prepare a bull for a sacrifice and place it on an unlit pile of wood, and he would do the same. Each side could then pray and see who answered with fire.[7]

2

The prophets of Baal accepted Elijah's challenge and went first, praying earnestly all morning for fire to consume their offering. When nothing happened, Elijah began to taunt them, saying maybe Baal was hard of hearing or asleep or busy doing something else. The prophets became more frantic, slashing themselves until their blood flowed. As evening approached, it became obvious that Baal would not respond.[8]

3

Elijah went into action then, building an altar with twelve stones representing the tribes of Israel. After placing the wood and sacrifice on the altar, Elijah called for barrels of water to be poured on it three times. Then he prayed, asking God to show his power to the people that their hearts might be turned to him again. Fire came down from heaven, burning up the sacrifice and everything else around it. When the people saw this, they

---

[5] 1 Kings 17:17-24
[6] 1 Kings 18:1-20
[7] 1 Kings 18:21-26
[8] 1 Kings 18:27-30

shouted, "The LORD is God! The LORD is God!"[9]

Elijah told the people to arrest the prophets of Baal and execute them. Then he told Ahab to go back to his palace before the coming deluge made his chariot useless. Elijah was filled with power and ran ahead of the king's chariot all the way back.[10]

When Ahab told Jezebel what had happened, she was furious, vowing that she would do to Elijah the same as he had done to her prophets. When Elijah heard of her threats, he went far into the desert where he prayed that he might die. An angel came to him with bread and water, telling him to eat and rest because this had been too much for him. Refreshed and encouraged, Elijah traveled south for forty days until he came to the mountain where God had given the Ten Commandments to Moses.[11]

God asked why he had come to the desert and Elijah replied that his greatest efforts had met with little success. The Israelites had rejected God's covenant and gone so far as to wage war on God's prophets. Elijah was feeling alone and helpless.[12]

4 Elijah stood to his feet when told God was about to appear to him. A mighty storm shook the mountain, but Elijah could see that God was not in the storm. Next came an earthquake, but God was not in the earthquake. Then came a roaring fire, but God was not in the fire. Finally, in the eerie silence that followed these spectacular outbursts, there came a gentle whisper. Elijah then covered his face with a cloak because he knew he was in the presence of God.[13]

God asked again what was wrong and Elijah repeated his complaint: despite his best efforts, Elijah felt alone and helpless in stopping the Israelites from going down the path they had chosen. God told Elijah to go back because there would be a new

---

[9] 1 Kings 18:31-39

[10] 1 Kings 18:40-46

[11] 1 Kings 19:1-9

[12] 1 Kings 19:10-11

[13] 1 Kings 19:11-13

king to anoint and a new prophet to call. God also said there were 7,000 people who had remained faithful to the LORD in the midst of these difficult times.[14]

As Elijah returned, he came upon Elisha, a wealthy farmer who was plowing his fields with twelve pairs of oxen. Elijah said nothing, but placed his cloak upon Elisha and continued walking. Elisha understood the significance of what Elijah had done and ran after him to ask if he could say farewell to his family. Elisha symbolized an end to his former life by killing his oxen and sacrificing them on a fire made from burning his plow. Leaving all behind, Elisha became Elijah's disciple.[15]

While Elijah was on his journey, the king of Aram besieged Samaria, Israel's capital city, and ordered King Ahab to surrender not only his gold and silver, but also his wives. Ahab initially agreed, but balked when the king of Aram demanded that his officials be allowed to search the king's palace to make certain nothing was held back. Ahab refused and prepared for war.[16]

A prophet came to Ahab and told him that God would give him victory over this vast army to show Ahab that the LORD is God. Ahab was skeptical, but sent his army to attack. The king of Aram was completely caught off guard and most of his men were drunk because they never imagined that Ahab's small army would attack their huge one. As Ahab's army began to inflict great losses, the king of Aram's army went into full retreat.[17]

Back home in Aram, the king tried to figure out what happened. His advisers told him the army lost because Ahab's army was aided by "the god of the hills." They encouraged him to raise another army to attack the next spring, this time fighting on the plains instead of the hills. The king of Aram became convinced

---

[14] 1 Kings 19:13-18
[15] 1 Kings 19:19-21
[16] 1 Kings 20:1-11
[17] 1 Kings 20:12-21

that such a strategy would render Israel's god powerless.[18]

The next spring, the two armies faced each other on the plains. Although the army of the Israelites looked pitifully small, a prophet had assured King Ahab that God would make them victorious in order to show the king of Aram that the power of the LORD was neither limited nor localized. The Israelites were victorious and the king of Aram barely escaped. Ahab negotiated a peace treaty with him.[19]

A prophet approached Ahab with a parable that showed it was not in the king's power to negotiate peace on his own terms. After all, the victory was God's, not Ahab's, and the fate of the king of Aram was in God's hands, not Ahab's. The prophet said Ahab would surely pay the price one day for his arrogance.[20]

Ahab's arrogance paled in comparison to that of Queen Jezebel. The king coveted a small piece of land near his palace for a garden. The owner, Naboth, rejected the king's reasonable offer, saying these were ancestral lands that were not for sale. The king became sullen and angry, whining and refusing to eat.[21]

Jezebel asked Ahab what was wrong and he told her how disappointed he was at not being able to get the land he wanted. She called him a weakling, and sent a letter in the king's name asking local officials to call a meeting at which two men would say the owner of the vineyard had cursed God and the king. The testimony of two witnesses would be sufficient to have the man stoned to death.[22]

Jezebel's plan was carried out and Ahab got the vineyard he wanted, but when he went to take possession of it, Elijah confronted him. Ahab's fate was sealed: he and Jezebel would die cruel, dishonorable deaths along with everyone else in his

---

[18] 1 Kings 20:22-25

[19] 1 Kings 20:26-34

[20] 1 Kings 20:35-43

[21] 1 Kings 21:1-4

[22] 1 Kings 21:5-10

family. The house of Ahab would end as the house of Jeroboam had years before.[23]

Devastated by what Elijah told him, Ahab entered a period of mourning and fasting. God told Elijah that because Ahab had humbled himself in this way, the judgment against his family would take place, but not until after the king's death.[24]

Back in Judah, Asa's son, Jehoshaphat, had become king. In the early part of his reign, he was faithful to the Torah, even to the point of sending teachers throughout Judah to instruct people in what the Torah said. The worst thing he did was to arrange a marriage with Athaliah, the daughter of Ahab and Jezebel.[25]

Ahab honored his peace treaty with the king of Aram for three years, but then decided he should retake some of Israel's land that had been lost earlier. Ahab sent messengers to the king of Judah to ask him to join in such an effort. Jehoshaphat agreed, requiring only that they ask the prophets to inquire whether God would give them victory.[26]

Ahab gathered hundreds of his prophets and asked if God would bring victory to the Israelites. The prophets were enthusiastic in their assurance that such would be the case, but the king of Judah was still not sure. "Is there not a prophet of the LORD in Israel?" he asked King Ahab, who replied that Micaiah hadn't been invited because he always brought bad news.[27]

At the urging of Jehoshaphat, Ahab sent a messenger for Micaiah. The messenger asked him to bring a good word to the king, but Micaiah responded he could only say what the LORD told him to say. Nevertheless, when asked by Ahab if God would bring victory, Micaiah told him what he wanted to hear. Knowing this was too good to be true, Ahab asked Micaiah to

---

[23] 1 Kings 21:11-26

[24] 1 Kings 21:27-29

[25] 2 Chronicles 17:1-19; 2 Chronicles 18:1

[26] 1 Kings 22:1-5; 2 Chronicles 18:2-4

[27] 1 Kings 22:6-12; 2 Chronicles 18:5-7

tell him what would really happen.[28]

Micaiah told Ahab that the Israelites would be like sheep without a shepherd because their leader would be killed in battle. He went on to say that God was luring Ahab into this battle by putting a lying spirit in the king's prophets. When they heard this, the prophets were incensed and attacked Micaiah and the king put Micaiah in prison.[29]

Having been warned by Micaiah that his life was at risk, Ahab devised a plan. He convinced Jehoshaphat to enter battle wearing royal armor while Ahab dressed as a common soldier. The ruse worked for a while, but the soldiers chasing Jehoshaphat turned away when they realized he was not the king of Israel. A random arrow struck Ahab and mortally wounded him. When the Israelites realized they had lost their king, they fled in retreat.[30]

Jehoshaphat returned to Jerusalem, and was chastised by a prophet for his alliance with Ahab. Jehoshaphat was told he would not be destroyed, though, because he had been faithful to God in removing idols. Jehoshaphat went on to implement legal reforms to see that justice was carried out among the people.[31]

5 Some time later, Judah was invaded by powerful armies from the eastern lands. Jehoshaphat proclaimed a fast to seek help from the LORD and received this message from God: "Do not fear; the battle is not yours, but God's! Take up your positions, stand firm, and watch the LORD deliver you."[32]

Jehoshaphat sent out his army, preceded by singers who loudly proclaimed, "Give thanks to the LORD whose love endures forever." As the army took its position, it discovered the enemy must have become crazed and destroyed each other. Judah's army collected much plunder and returned in triumph to

---

[28] 1 Kings 22:13-16; 2 Chronicles 18:8-15

[29] 1 Kings 22:17-28; 2 Chronicles 18:16-27

[30] 1 Kings 22:29-36; 2 Chronicles 18:28-34

[31] 2 Chronicles 19:1-11

[32] 2 Chronicles 20:1-17

Jerusalem. Fear spread throughout the region when it became known that God was fighting on Judah's behalf.[33]

Back in Israel, Ahab's son, who was now the king, had a nasty fall and sent messengers to the Philistines to ask the prophets of Baal whether he would recover. Elijah met the messengers soon after they began their journey and asked them, "Is there no god in Israel that you must go to the Philistines?" Elijah sent the messengers back with a message for Ahab's son: "You will never leave the bed on which you lie."[34]

Knowing this message must have come from Elijah, the king sent a captain with fifty soldiers to bring Elijah back. The captain found Elijah on the mountain, and ordered him to come down, but Elijah called down fire from heaven and the soldiers all died. The king sent another company of soldiers and the same thing happened. The captain of the third company of soldiers approached Elijah differently. Instead of demanding that Elijah come by order of the king, the captain asked Elijah to have mercy on him and spare his soldiers. God told Elijah to go with this man. Elijah confirmed to the king his message from God, and the king soon died with no son to succeed him.[35]

When Elijah knew the end of his life was at hand, he told **6** Elisha to stay behind, but Elisha repeatedly insisted on going with him. As the two of them traveled, companies of prophets came and asked if Elisha knew that God was about to take Elijah from him. Elisha said he knew, and asked them not to talk about it.[36]

When Elijah reached the river, he took off his cloak and struck the water with it. After the water parted and they had crossed to the other side, Elisha asked if he could inherit a double portion of Elijah's spirit. Elijah said such a request was not his to grant, but if Elisha saw him taken up to heaven, he would know his

---

[33] 2 Chronicles 20:18-30

[34] 2 Kings 1:1-6

[35] 2 Kings 1:7-22

[36] 2 Kings 2:1-7

request had been granted.[37]

As they were talking, a chariot of fire came between them and Elisha saw Elijah ascend to heaven in a whirlwind. Elisha picked up the cloak that Elijah had dropped and struck the river with it. As the waters parted, Elisha knew his request had been granted. Other miracles followed.[38]

Another of Ahab's sons became king of Israel and faced war with the Moabites. He asked the king of Judah to join him, and Jehoshaphat agreed to do so. As the armies were traveling, they ran out of water and thought they might die in the desert before they ever saw the enemy. Jehoshaphat asked if there was any prophet nearby who could intercede with God on their behalf.[39]

The kings approached Elisha, who asked them why they weren't turning to the prophets of Baal, whom Ahab and Jezebel had so favored. "We come to you because it is the LORD God who sent us on this mission," the king of Israel replied. Elisha was still not impressed, but said he would inquire of God for the sake of Jehoshaphat, the king of Judah.[40]

Elisha asked them to bring a harpist, and as he was listening to the music, God told him the soldiers should dig ditches because water would soon flow into them. God also told Elisha the kings would be successful when the battle with the Moabites began.[41]

The morning after the ditches were completed, water indeed began to flow into them. As the Moabite army approached early the next morning, the sunlight shining on the water looked to them like blood. Thinking that the armies of Israel and Judah must have slaughtered each other, the Moabites rushed in for plunder. How surprised they were to find the armies refreshed

---

[37] 2 Kings 2:8-10

[38] 2 Kings 2:11-25

[39] 2 Kings 3:1-11

[40] 2 Kings 3:12-14

[41] 2 Kings 3:15-19

and ready for battle![42]

The Moabites fled and were pursued by the armies of Israel and Judah all the way to Moab. As the Moabite losses mounted, their king sacrificed his firstborn son on the city wall in a desperate attempt to gain his god's favor, but it was to no avail.[43]

Elisha met a prophet's widow who could only pay her debts by selling her sons into slavery. Elisha asked if she had any resources at all and she told him she had only one small flask of oil. He told her to borrow as many jars from her neighbors as she could and fill them with oil. The oil stopped flowing when the last jar was full and she had enough to pay her debts.[44]

Elisha met another woman who invited him to her home for dinner. The woman and her husband asked him to come again, and eventually prepared a room for him to use whenever he was in the area. Elisha asked the woman if there was something he could do for her in return, but she said she needed nothing. Elisha's servant commented that the woman had everything except a son, and there was little hope of her ever having one because of her husband's age.[45]

When Elisha told her she would have a son in the coming year, she replied that he should not tease her, but the next year a son was born and the couple was delighted. After some time passed, the child told his father he had a severe headache; before the day was over, the child died resting on his mother's lap. She put the child on the bed in Elisha's room and went to see the prophet.[46]

As the woman approached, Elisha knew something was wrong. The grieving woman said to him, "Did I ask for a son? Did I not warn you not to raise my hopes?" She told him all that had happened and Elisha told his servant to run to the child and place

---

[42] 2 Kings 3:20-24

[43] 2 Kings 3:25-27

[44] 2 Kings 4:1-7

[45] 2 Kings 4:8-14

[46] 2 Kings 4:15-25

Elisha's staff on the boy's body. The servant did as Elisha requested, but when the prophet arrived at the home, nothing had changed. Elisha went into the room and stretched out on the child, sensing the child's body growing warm as he did so. Elisha stretched out on him again and the boy woke up sneezing. Elisha gave the boy back to his mother.[47]

One day Elisha was invited to have dinner with a company of prophets, one of whom cut up some unknown wild gourds and put them in a stew. The cook realized the stew had become poisonous and told everyone not to eat it, but Elisha threw some flour in the stew and it became safe to eat.[48]

On another occasion, Elisha was brought twenty loaves of fresh bread. When he told his servants to feed the people with it, they replied that much more bread would be needed to feed so many. He assured them the bread would be sufficient and that some would be leftover as well. It happened just as Elisha said.[49]

Naaman, the commander of a foreign army, was a good man and a valiant soldier who had leprosy. His wife's servant, captured in a raid on the Israelites, told of a prophet in Israel who could cure him. When Naaman heard this, he asked his king to send a gift and write a letter to the king of Israel. The letter simply said, "Please see that Naaman is cured of his leprosy."[50]

The king of Israel tore his robes when he received the letter, saying, "Am I a god that I can cure leprosy?" Elisha sent the king a message: "Have Naaman come to me and I will show him the power of God." When Naaman arrived at his door, Elisha sent a servant outside to tell Naaman to wash seven times in the Jordan River and his leprosy would be gone."[51]

Naaman was angry. Elisha had done nothing to effect a cure, and

---

[47] 2 Kings 4:26-37
[48] 2 Kings 4:38-41
[49] 2 Kings 4:42-44
[50] 2 Kings 5:1-6
[51] 2 Kings 5:7-10

had not even shown Naaman the courtesy of coming out to greet him. Naaman's servants calmed him down, reminding him that he had been willing to do something difficult at the suggestion of Elijah. Should he not also be willing to do something simple? Naaman saw the wisdom of what they were saying, did as Elisha had told him, and was healed.[52]

Naaman returned to Elisha, insisting on giving him a lavish gift in gratitude for his healing. When Elisha refused, Naaman asked if Elisha would allow him to take home as much soil as two donkeys could carry. He told Elisha this would allow him to worship the LORD on Israelite soil because it was his intention never to worship any other god from that point forward with one exception: when Naaman entered a foreign temple with the king and the king bowed down, he would have to bow as well to avoid offending the king. Elisha told Naaman to go in peace.[53]

After Naaman had left, Elisha's servant followed him and asked for money and clothing for two prophets in need. Naaman gladly obliged and the servant returned and hid what he had been given. Elisha asked the servant where he had gone and the man said he had not gone anywhere. Elisha said he had seen everything that had happened. For deceit and covetousness, the servant would be punished: the leprosy that had been taken from Naaman would now come upon him and there would be no hope of healing.[54]

The prophets who met regularly with Elisha complained to him one day that they had outgrown their quarters. He told them to cut down some trees for a new building and went with them as they did so. While cutting down a tree near the river, one of the men lost the head of an axe he was using. He became distraught when he saw the axe disappear, because it had been borrowed and he had no means of paying for its loss. Elisha came to the spot where the axe head had fallen in the water and threw a stick in after it. The axe head came to the surface and was retrieved,

---

[52] 2 Kings 5:11-14
[53] 2 Kings 5:15-19
[54] 2 Kings 5:20-27

saving the man who lost it from having to become a slave.[55]

The king of Aram decided to attack Israel, but realized his best chance of success would come if he could set up an ambush. Every trap failed because the Israelites seemed to know exactly where he would be. The king thought there must be a traitor among his inner circle until he was told by one of his officers that it was Elisha who warned the Israelites of what was coming. "He knows your every thought," the king was told.[56]

7 The king sent a small army to capture Elisha, but his plans were frustrated once again when Elisha prayed that God would blind the soldiers with a dazzling light. Elisha then offered to lead the dazed soldiers to find the man they sought. The next thing the soldiers knew, they were in Samaria standing before the king of Israel who wanted to execute them on the spot. Elisha said the king could not dispose of them because it was not the king who had captured them. Elisha said it would be better to give them a feast and send them on their way. The king agreed, choosing hospitality over vengeance and bringing peace to Israel.[57]

The peace lasted for a time, but eventually a new king in Aram decided once again to attack Israel. Rather than doing so by stealth as before, this king laid siege to Samaria and waited for its inhabitants to starve or surrender. Lack of food in the city led people to desperate acts. One woman approached the king of Israel to ask for his help; she and another woman had agreed to eat their children, but the other woman had hid her own child after the first was gone. Would the king force this woman to bring her child forward as agreed?[58]

Distraught by such a turn of events, the king turned his anger against Elisha. He and his men stormed into Elisha's home, determined to kill him, but Elisha said if the king would wait one

[55] 2 Kings 6:1-7
[56] 2 Kings 6:8-12
[57] 2 Kings 6:13-23
[58] 2 Kings 6:24-29

day, he would discover how plentiful food had become. The king and his men scoffed at Elisha's words, but decided to wait.[59]

Four men with leprosy were staying at the gate of the city and becoming desperate as well. They decided there was no hope for them within the city and they might as well surrender to the Aramean army. When they arrived at the camp, they were surprised to find it empty. They had no way of knowing that God had sent a spirit of fear and madness into the army, and they had fled into the night leaving everything behind.[60]

The lepers were enjoying their good fortune when they realized the news should be shared with those in the city. When the king of Israel heard the lepers' story, he suspected a trap. Then a number of his own soldiers discovered that the story was true, and the king opened the gates, letting people storm through them to take what had been left in the enemy's camp. As Elisha had predicted, there was more than enough for everyone.[61]

The king of Aram became ill and sent one of his officials, Hazael, to ask whether he would recover. Elisha said, "You may tell the king he will live, but he will not." Then Elisha began to weep. When Hazael asked him why, Elisha told him it was because he had foreseen the atrocities Hazael would commit against the Israelites when he came into power. Bolstered by this prophecy, Hazael returned and told the king that he would live, but the next day found opportunity to suffocate him and have himself declared king.[62]

The time had come for Elisha to carry out the last part of Elijah's mission by anointing a man named Jehu to be king of Israel and encouraging him to wipe out all that was left of Ahab's family. Elisha sent another prophet to anoint Jehu while the king of Israel was recovering from battle wounds. Because he commanded the army, Jehu's anointing was welcomed by his

---

[59] 2 Kings 6:30-33; 2 Kings 7:1-2

[60] 2 Kings 7:3-7

[61] 2 Kings 7:8-20

[62] 2 Kings 8:8-15

men, and they set off to destroy the house of Ahab.[63]

The king of Israel, accompanied by his new ally, the king of Judah, met Jehu at the vineyard Jezebel had acquired for Ahab by having its owner falsely accused and executed. The king of Israel discovered too late that Jehu had not come in peace. Jehu announced his intention and shot the king of Israel in the back as he was fleeing. The king of Judah was wounded as well, but escaped with his life.[64]

Jehu returned to the city to confront Jezebel, who was looking out a window as they came. When Jehu announced his intentions, Jezebel's servants threw her out the window to her death. Then Jehu sent letters to the officials that they should either anoint one of Ahab's seventy descendants to be king or else bring their heads to Jehu. Terrified by Jehu's wrath, the officials chose to sacrifice the seventy men and the house of Ahab was no more.[65]

Next Jehu turned his wrath on Judah, which had been aligned with Israel ever since its former king had married Athaliah, the daughter of Ahab and Jezebel. Jehu put to death the king of Judah and as much of his family as could be found.[66]

Finally, Jehu dealt with the prophets of Baal. He announced a great feast in honor of Baal that would demonstrate his determination to be even more devoted to Baal than Ahab had been. All the prophets and priests of Baal were told attendance at this festival was mandatory and all complied. When they arrived, each guest was given a special robe identifying them as a prophet or priest of Baal. Jehu then commanded his palace guard to kill everyone wearing one of the special robes. When the massacre was complete, the soldiers tore down the temple and

---

[63] 2 Kings 9:1-13

[64] 2 Kings 9:15-27

[65] 2 Kings 9:30-37; 2 Kings 10:1-11

[66] 2 Kings 10:12-17; 2 Kings 11:1; 2 Chronicles 22:8-10

turned it into a latrine.[67]

In spite of Jehu's zeal in destroying the prophets of Baal, in other ways he was sorely lacking. He showed little respect for the Torah, and continued to worship the golden calves that Jeroboam had installed at Bethel and Dan. Even with these major flaws, Jehu's descendants would thrive, ruling Israel for the next hundred years.[68]

[67] 2 Kings 10:18-27
[68] 2 Kings 10:28-36; 2 Kings 13:1-25

Questions for Reflection/Discussion

1. Worshipping the god of rain led to no rain. Is this like someone today ending up bankrupt after worshipping money? Can you think of other examples of life's irony in this regard?

2. Elijah told the Israelites they would have to choose because worshipping both Baal and the LORD God was not an option. What things do people 'worship' in today's world that are incompatible with being faithful to God?

3. Elijah taunted the prophets of Baal as they were trying to bring down fire from heaven. Does this feel intolerant and disrespectful to you? Are there situations in which it would be appropriate to mock another person's religion?

4. God appeared to Elijah as a still small voice. Think of a situation in which you felt God's presence. What was it like?

5. Jehoshaphat was told, "The battle is not yours, but God's." Are there battles today that God fights on our behalf? When is it presumptuous to think that God is on our side?

6. Elisha persisted in following Elijah even when he was told to stay behind. Have you ever persisted in pursuing something when others encouraged you to stop? How did it turn out?

7. Elisha broke the cycle of violence by encouraging the king to have a feast for the captured soldiers rather than having them executed. What would happen if we tried something like this in today's conflicts?

CHAPTER 11:
THE FALL OF ISRAEL

After the king of Judah had been killed in Jehu's purge, his mother, Athaliah, asserted her right to be queen. She made certain there would be no rivals to her throne by having the rest of her family put to death.[1]

Or at least she thought she did. Joash, the infant son of the king had been hidden in the Temple by priests during the queen's murderous rampage. When Joash was seven years old, the high priest, Jehoiada, decided it was time to anoint him king. Jehoiada brought the commanders of the army into his confidence and stationed them near the Temple. After Joash was anointed and came out of the Temple, he was greeted by shouts of "Long live the king!"[2]

Athaliah heard the uproar and came to investigate. When she realized what had happened, she shouted, "Treason, treason!" The high priest was prepared for this, having ordered the army to kill the queen and anyone who stood with her. From that point on, Jehoiada ruled through Joash until the king was old enough to rule on his own. The high priest ordered the temple of Baal to be destroyed, and led the people to reaffirm the Torah.[3]

When Joash came of age, he decided to renew the LORD's Temple in Jerusalem. He asked the priests to oversee the project and use some of the Temple offerings to pay for it. After eight years had passed with little accomplished by the priests, Joash had others collect the offerings and rebuild the Temple.[4]

After the death of Jehoiada, the high priest who had guided him from the beginning, King Joash lost his bearings and followed his people into apostasy. God sent warnings through prophets, but neither Joash nor the people listened. Even when Jehoiada's

---

[1] 2 Kings 8:25-29; 9:27-29; 2 Chronicles 22:1-10
[2] 2 Kings 11:4-12; 2 Chronicles 23:1-11
[3] 2 Kings 11:17-21; 12:1-3; 2 Chronicles 23:16-21; 24:1-2
[4] 2 Kings 12:4-16; 2 Chronicles 24:3-14

own son brought a message of warning, the people rejected his words and stoned him to death.[5]

Problems came quickly for Joash after that. The king of Aram attacked Jerusalem and Joash was wounded in battle. He surrendered, agreeing to give many items of value from the Temple and the palace in order to spare the city. Not much later, Joash was assassinated by some of his officials while recovering from wounds he had received in battle. As soon as his son, Amaziah, was anointed king, he avenged his father's death.[6]

The new king next prepared for a threatened attack by the Edomites. Fearing that his army was too small, Amaziah hired a large number of troops from Israel. A prophet told Amaziah this was a mistake, and the king dismissed the hired troops. God gave Amaziah victory over the Edomites, allowing him to win back all the land that originally belonged to Judah.[7]

Amaziah's victory was not without its problems. The troops from Israel that he had dismissed were angry that they had not shared in the plunder as victors. To gain revenge, they attacked several cities of Judah. Amaziah asked for a face-to-face conference with the king of Israel to discuss the situation.[8]

The king of Israel arrogantly said that such a conversation would be like a lowly thorn bush speaking to a regal cedar tree. Instead he met the king of Judah on the field of battle and soundly defeated him. Amaziah was allowed to live, but part of Jerusalem's wall was torn down and more treasures from the Temple and palace were taken. Amaziah lived another fifteen years after this defeat, but was then assassinated like his father.[9]

Amaziah's son, Uzziah, became king of Judah when he was sixteen years old. In the beginning, he sought the LORD and

---

[5] 2 Chronicles 24:15-22

[6] 2 Kings 12:17-21; 14:1-6; 2 Chronicles 24:23-27; 25:1-4

[7] 2 Chronicles 25:5-16

[8] 2 Kings 14:7-8; 2 Chronicles 25:1-4

[9] 2 Kings 14:9-20; 2 Chronicles 25:17-28

prospered, but as he grew strong, he also grew proud and suffered the consequences. Uzziah entered the Temple at one point, determined to offer his own sacrifices. When the priest confronted him with this violation of the Torah, Uzziah became angry. He also became leprous and remained so for the remainder of his life. Because Uzziah's leprosy prevented him from leaving the palace, his son, Jothan, ruled in his place.[10]

These four kings, Joash, Amaziah, Uzziah, and Jothan, reigned in Judah for a century (835-735 BCE). During roughly that same period, four generations of the House of Jehu reigned in Israel. It was during this period that Amos, Hosea and Isaiah were called by God to confront Judah and Israel with their sins.

The reign of Jeroboam II, the last of the House of Jehu, was singled out for criticism by the prophet Amos because of its arrogant immorality. Their sexual immorality was such that fathers and sons were sleeping with the same young women. Their economic immorality was no less outrageous: [2]

They trample on the heads of the poor
as upon the dust of the ground
and deny justice to the oppressed.[11]

Amos also confronted those who were wealthy, telling them they should not expect to enjoy the riches they gained from exploiting the poor. The rich might build mansions, but they would not live in them for long because a time of judgment was coming.[12]

Amos said Israel's problem was not that it lacked religion – it just had the wrong kind of religion, a false one that failed to produce the kind of relationships called for in the Torah. God rejected this kind of empty religion in no uncertain terms: [3]

I hate, I despise your religious festivals;
I cannot stand your assemblies.
Even though you bring me burnt offerings

---

[10] 2 Kings 15:1-6; 2 Chronicles 26:1-23
[11] Amos 2:6-8 (TNIV)
[12] Amos 5:11-12

and grain offerings, I will not accept them.
Away with the noise of your songs!
I will not listen to the music of your harps.
But let justice roll on like a river,
righteousness like a never-failing stream![13]

4 How had Israel ended up in such a condition? Amos said the fault lay with the king and all those who were responsible for the people's welfare. They were too absorbed in their own pleasure to take note of what was happening to their country:

You rich people lounge around on beds with ivory posts,
while dining on the meat of your lambs and calves.
You sing foolish songs to the music of harps,
and you make up new tunes, just as David used to do.
You drink all the wine you want
and wear expensive perfume,
but you don't care about the ruin of your nation.[14]

During this time, the Assyrian Empire was growing immensely powerful, destroying any country that refused to pay tribute and swear allegiance. The Assyrians invaded in 738 BCE, agreeing to spare Israel only if they paid tons of silver for the 'privilege' of being a loyal vassal of the Assyrian Empire. Israel believed a day was coming when God would deliver them, but Amos said their hopes were misplaced – Israel was about to experience judgment, not deliverance. The day of the LORD was coming, but it would be a time of darkness, not light.[15]

Paying tribute to Assyria created financial hardships for Israel. Unfortunately, this led to increased exploitation of the poor by the rich. Amos noted how the wealthy were "skimping the measure, boosting the price, and cheating with dishonest scales."

---

[13] Amos 5:21-24 (TNIV)

[14] Amos 6:1-6 (CEV)

[15] 2 Kings 15:19-21; Amos 5:18-20

Such outrageous behavior did not go unnoticed by God.[16]

God's prophets confronted not only Israel, but its enemies as well. Jonah was told by God to deliver a message of judgment to Nineveh, the capital city of Assyria. News of Nineveh's fate was welcomed by Jonah except for one thing: he was convinced that if the people repented, God would forgive them rather than destroy them. To keep this from happening, Jonah went as far from Nineveh as he could.[17]

Jonah was on a ship when a violent storm erupted. Jonah realized what was happening and told the sailors to throw him overboard rather than lose their lives along with his. After exhausting other options, they did so, and Jonah was rescued by a huge fish. After three days and nights in the belly of the fish, Jonah was cast upon the shore.[18]

Jonah was told once again to go to Nineveh and this time he obeyed. When the people of Nineveh heard Jonah's message, they repented of the evil they had done. As Jonah had feared, God forgave the people of Nineveh rather than destroying the city and its entire population as threatened.[19]

This left Jonah profoundly angry that Israel's God would show love and compassion to Israel's enemies. God appeared to Jonah in an attempt to show him how wrong-headed his desire for vengeance was, but Jonah remained unconvinced.[20]

About this same time, Isaiah was called by God to be a prophet who would confront Israel with its sins, a task for which he felt totally unqualified:

> *Then I cried out, "I'm doomed! Everything I say is sinful, and so are the words of everyone around me. Yet I have seen the King, the LORD All-Powerful."*

---

[16] Amos 8:4-12
[17] Jonah 1:1-3; 4:1-2
[18] Jonah 1:4-17; 2:1-10
[19] Jonah 3:1-10
[20] Jonah 4:3-11

> *One of the flaming creatures flew over to me with a burning coal that it had taken from the altar with a pair of metal tongs. It touched my lips with the hot coal and said, "This has touched your lips. Your sins are forgiven, and you are no longer guilty."*
>
> *After this, I heard the LORD ask, "Is there anyone I can send? Will someone go for us?"*
>
> *"I'll go," I answered. "Send me!"* [21]

Isaiah's ministry was never an easy one because God made it clear to him from the beginning that people would not respond to his message. Their hearts would be hardened and their minds dull until the country lay in ruins and the people had been carried away to foreign lands.[22]

6 Prophets were called to convey God's message to people through various means. The prophet Hosea, for instance, spoke through what he did as well as through what he said. Hosea's first prophetic act was to marry an adulterous woman whose behavior symbolized Israel's unfaithfulness to God. Their first child was named 'Jezreel' because in the valley of Jezreel, Israel would be defeated. Their second child was called 'Unloved' because God would no longer show love to Israel. Their third child was called 'Not My People' because God had rejected the Israelites.[23]

Israel's political situation was in turmoil during this time as Pekah, a captain in the army, assassinated the king and assumed the throne. The fact that five of the six previous kings of Israel had been assassinated set the stage for Israel's ultimate demise. During Pekah's reign, the Assyrians invaded again and captured much of northern Israel, taking everyone in those areas back to Assyria.[24]

---

[21] Isaiah 6:1-8 (CEV)

[22] Isaiah 6:9-13

[23] Hosea 1:2-9; 2:16-19

[24] 2 Kings 15:22-31

Isaiah prophesied that this was more than a minor setback for the leaders of Israel, who could not expect things to go well as long as they made unjust laws that took advantage of widows and orphans, and deprived the poor and vulnerable of their right to justice. Those who did such things should realize that a day of reckoning would come and bring disaster with it.[25]

The problem with the Israelites was that they had their priorities all wrong:

> *Woe to those who are heroes at drinking wine*
>   *and champions at mixing drinks,*
> *who acquit the guilty for a bribe,*
>   *but deny justice to the innocent.*[26]

The destruction of Israel was inevitable because leaders who should have given warning refused to see what was happening.

> *For the leaders of my people—*
>   *the LORD's watchmen, his shepherds—*
>   *are blind and ignorant.*
> *They are like silent watchdogs*
>   *that give no warning when danger comes.*
> *They love to lie around, sleeping and dreaming.*[27]

While Israel was plummeting toward destruction, Judah was having its share of problems as well. Jotham's son, Ahaz, became king and reigned in Jerusalem for sixteen years. Ahaz worshipped false gods, going so far as to sacrifice his son by fire to a Canaanite god. Ahaz also replaced the altar in God's Temple with one based on a design he had seen in Damascus.[28]

The kings of Israel and Aram joined forces to attack Judah in hopes of forcing Judah to be an ally in their rebellion against Assyria. The situation looked hopeless for Judah until Isaiah came to King Ahaz with a word of encouragement: Judah would

---

[25] Isaiah 9:8-10; 10:1-4

[26] Isaiah 5:22-25 (TNIV)

[27] Isaiah 56:10-12 (NLT)

[28] 2 Kings 16:1-4

suffer, but would not be destroyed by Israel and Aram. Because Ahaz remained unconvinced, Isaiah reassured him:

> *All right then, the Lord himself will give you the sign. Look! The virgin will conceive a child! She will give birth to a son and will call him Immanuel (which means 'God is with us'). By the time this child is old enough to choose what is right and reject what is wrong, he will be eating yogurt and honey. For before the child is that old, the lands of the two kings you fear so much will both be deserted.*[29]

When the attack by Israel and Aram came, many in Judah died and others were taken in captivity to Samaria. The prophet Oded, however, confronted Israel's king with a warning that something far worse would come on Israel if they enslaved their Jewish kin. King Pekah relented, clothing the naked captives and sending them home.[30]

To prevent further attacks by Israel and Aram, Judah turned to Assyria for help, but their request for an alliance was met by an attack. The only way Judah could survive the Assyrian assault was by agreeing to pay tribute. King Ahaz gave everything of value in the Temple to the Assyrian king and then closed the doors of the Temple. From then on, Ahaz allowed sacrifices to be made only to the gods of Damascus.[31]

King Pekah had little time to gloat over Judah's fate because he was assassinated by a man named Hoshea, who soon decided to break free from Assyrian domination and enter into an alliance with Egypt. Isaiah warned that such an alliance was foolish.[32]

When the Assyrian king realized the king of Israel was not paying his tribute, the Assyrian army was sent to teach them a lesson. Samaria was besieged by the Assyrians and held out for

---

[29] 2 Kings 16:5-6; Isaiah 7:1-17 (NLT)

[30] 2 Chronicles 28:1-15

[31] 2 Kings 16:7-20; 28:16-27

[32] Isaiah 31:1

three years before surrendering. Most of the inhabitants of Israel were deported to Assyria and scattered throughout the empire.[33]

Israel was repopulated with inhabitants from other nations by order of the Assyrians. When the new settlers encountered problems, the king of Assyria was told it was because they did not know the god of that land. He sent a captured priest back to them in order that they might learn to worship the God of Israel. Unfortunately, the priest who was sent knew only the distorted version of worship that had been practiced in Israel since the days of Jeroboam. The Samaritans thus ended up with a syncretistic religion, combining what they already knew along with what the Israelite priest taught them.[34]

Although God used the Assyrians as an instrument of wrath against the Israelites, a day of reckoning was coming for the Assyrians as well. God told Isaiah, "I will punish the king of Assyria for the willful pride of his heart and the haughty look in his eyes." The Assyrian king had boasted that it was by his own strength and wisdom that he had brought other nations to their knees. He would soon learn otherwise.[35]

---

[33] 2 Kings 17:1-23
[34] 2 Kings 17:24-41
[35] Isaiah 10:5-19 (TNIV)

Questions for Reflection/Discussion

1. After murdering all rivals to the throne, Athaliah accused Joash and his supporters of treason. This sounds like an example of "what goes around comes around." What are some other examples of people whose mistreatment of others came back to haunt them?

2. Amos confronted Israel because of its sexual and economic immorality. Do you agree that denying justice to the poor should be considered immoral? How do you define immorality?

3. Amos said the Israelites were foolish to think that God would accept their worship when their country was full of injustice. Do churches today often avoid issues of justice in order to focus on spiritual matters? Why do you think they do this?

4. Israel suffered because its leaders showed little concern for anything except their own luxury and pleasure. What portion of our national and world leaders today act similarly? What about bosses, managers and corporate executives? Who suffers when leaders act like this?

5. Jonah was upset because God forgave those who Jonah knew had done terrible things. Which tends to upset you more: when the innocent suffer or when the guilty go unpunished? Do you become angry at God when either of these happens?

6. By marrying a woman of ill repute, Hosea delivered his prophetic message in a symbolic action as well as in words. How do people today use symbolic actions to communicate messages?

CHAPTER 12:
HEZEKIAH, MANASSEH, JOSIAH

Six years after the northern tribes of Israel had been carried away in captivity to Assyria, Hezekiah, another descendant of David, became king of Judah. His reign of nearly thirty years was characterized by faithfulness to the Torah such as had not been seen since the time of his ancestor King David. In the first year of Hezekiah's reign, he opened the door of the Temple, telling the priests to clean out the filth that had accumulated over the years and make repairs as necessary. The people rejoiced at what God had done to restore Temple worship.[1]

Hezekiah sent couriers throughout Judah to announce that Passover would once again be observed. He even invited those in Israel who had been left behind after the deportation to Assyria. Many within this remnant who received the invitation laughed with scorn, and others came to celebrate Passover without going through the required ritual cleansing. Hezekiah asked God to be gracious to the latter because their hearts were right even if their observance of the Torah was faulty. The week-long celebration was so well received that Hezekiah decided to prolong it for another week. Such a celebration had not been seen in Jerusalem since the time of Solomon, more than two hundred years earlier.[2]

When the celebration ended, the people began removing the worship centers of all the false gods throughout the country. After destroying the idols, altars, sacred stones, and Asherah poles, the people began worshipping the LORD in accordance with the Torah. The tithes and offerings they brought to the Temple were so generous that a surplus soon resulted.[3]

The prophet Micah, however, warned that such religious reforms would not fulfill the Torah unless accompanied by commitment to faithful living. God did not require enormous

1

---

[1] 2 Kings 17:18; 2 Chronicles 29:1-36
[2] 2 Chronicles 30:1-27
[3] 2 Chronicles 31:1-19

offerings, and certainly not the abominable practice of sacrificing children to atone for the sins of their parents.

> *The LORD God has told us what is right*
> *and what he demands:*
>> *See that justice is done,*
>> *let mercy be your first concern,*
>> *and humbly obey your God.*[4]

Things were going so well that Hezekiah decided to declare his independence from the king of Assyria. God was with Hezekiah in this, and also in the king's conquest of the Philistines who had encroached on the land of Judah during the reign of his predecessors. Isaiah celebrated the peace and prosperity that God had brought through Hezekiah as reason for confidence in what God would do in the future.[5]

> *For to us a child is born, to us a son is given,*
> *and the government will be on his shoulders.*
> *And he will be called Wonderful Counselor,*
>> *Mighty God, Everlasting Father, Prince of Peace.*
> *Of the increase of his government and peace*
>> *there will be no end.*
> *He will reign on David's throne and over his kingdom,*
>> *establishing and upholding it*
>> *with justice and righteousness*
>> *from that time on and forever.*[6]

Unfortunately, the peace and prosperity that came in Hezekiah's reign did not last long. Eight years after the fall of Israel, a new king of Assyria invaded Judah and captured some of its smaller towns. Hezekiah did what he could to defend Jerusalem. He repaired the city's walls and eliminated any sources of water that might be used by an army camped outside the city. Fearing that this would not be enough, Hezekiah sent large quantities of gold and silver to the Assyrians to appease them. But even this was

---

[4] Micah 6:6-8 (CEV)

[5] 2 Kings 18:4-8; 2 Chronicles 31:20-21

[6] Isaiah 9:2-7 (TNIV)

not enough. The Assyrians marched to Jerusalem and asked to meet with emissaries to explain that no god and no foreign ally could save the people of Judah.[7]

Inside the palace, King Hezekiah was seriously ill. After Isaiah came and told him to put his affairs in order because he would soon die, the king wept bitterly and asked God to remember how faithful he had been. Even before Isaiah had left the palace, another message came to him from the LORD. Isaiah returned to the king and told him fifteen years had been added to his life and Jerusalem would be spared as well. Hezekiah asked for a sign that this would truly happen and Isaiah granted his request: just as the word of Hezekiah's death was turned back, so would the king's clock be turned back ten hours.[8]

While all this was happening inside the palace, the Assyrians outside the gates were warning the Judeans that relying on the Egyptians was foolish for they were notoriously untrustworthy. The Judeans replied that their trust was in the LORD, not in Egypt. The Assyrians expressed their doubts about this as well, arguing that if Hezekiah was truly trusting in God, he would not have destroyed all the worship sites of the gods. The Assyrian leader said maybe these gods were sending him to punish Hezekiah because they were angry at what he had done.[9]

The Judean emissaries were so dismayed by what the Assyrians were saying that they asked if the discussions could be held in Aramaic, the language of diplomacy, rather than in Hebrew, which all the Judeans could understand. The Assyrians countered that everyone had a right to know the foolishness of Hezekiah's resistance because it was the people themselves who would suffer the effects of a siege.[10]

The Assyrians ridiculed the idea that God would save Judah because no god had yet been able to stand up to the

---

[7] 2 Kings 18:13-18; 2 Chronicles 32:1-8; Isaiah 22:1-14; 36:1-2

[8] 2 Kings 20:1-11; 2 Chronicles 32:24-26; Isaiah 38:1-8

[9] 2 Kings 18:19-25; 2 Chronicles 32:9-12; Isaiah 36:3-10

[10] 2 Kings 18:26-30; 2 Chronicles 32:17-19; Isaiah 36:11-12

might of the Assyrian empire. Furthermore, if the Judeans would only put their trust in the Assyrians, they would be taken to a new promised land where there would be food and water for all. The Judeans had a choice: trusting in God would bring death; trusting in the Assyrians would bring life.[11]

Hezekiah and all who heard had no response but to mourn their fate. The king sent word to the prophet Isaiah, asking if he might pray to God on their behalf. Isaiah told them not to worry because the LORD would send a message to the Assyrian king that would make him return home to meet his fate.[12]

Hezekiah received another warning from the Assyrians, this one in writing. He took the letter to the Temple and spread it out before God. As he prayed, Hezekiah affirmed that the LORD was not only the God of Judah, but of all the nations of the earth, including Assyria. Hezekiah asked God to save the Judeans to prove there was no other god, and that all the so-called gods were nothing more than useless pieces of wood and stone.[13]

Isaiah told Hezekiah that the Assyrian king was foolish to insult God. The success that the Assyrians had in conquering other nations was part of God's plan, and the downfall of the Assyrian king was another part of the same plan. Isaiah then assured Hezekiah that within three years, crops would again be harvested in Judah. The Assyrians would not take Jerusalem, because God would defend it for his own sake and for the sake of David.[14]

That night, a plague swept through the Assyrian army, killing thousands. The Assyrian king returned to his home, where two of his sons assassinated him and fled the country; another of his sons became king.[15]

Isaiah proclaimed that Judah should not take comfort from its

---

[11] 2 Kings 18:31-35; 2 Chronicles 32:13-16; Isaiah 36:13-20

[12] 2 Kings 18:36-37; 19:1-7; Isaiah 36:21-22; 37:1-7

[13] 2 Kings 19:8-19; Isaiah 37:8-20

[14] 2 Kings 19:20-35; Isaiah 37:21-35

[15] 2 Kings 19:36-37; 2 Chronicles 32:20-21; Isaiah 37:36-38

escape, for its situation was still precarious. Hezekiah's reforms had simply not gone far enough:

> *These people come near to me with their mouth*
> *and honor me with their lips,*
> *but their hearts are far from me.*[16]

Jerusalem's fate would be no better than that of Samaria [4] unless they began living faithfully as the Torah required. The Judeans had come to think that God was pleased by the devotion they showed in worship, but they could not have been more wrong:

> *Your sacrifices mean nothing to me.*
> *I am sick of your offering of rams and choice cattle;*
> *I don't like the blood of bulls or lambs or goats.*
> *Who asked you to bring all this*
> *when you come to worship me?*[17]

What God really wanted was for them to give up their [5] propensity for violence and begin showing compassion to those who were less fortunate.

> *No matter how much you pray, I won't listen.*
> *You are too violent.*
> *Wash yourselves clean!*
> *I am disgusted with your filthy deeds.*
> *Stop doing wrong and learn to live right.*
> *See that justice is done.*
> *Defend widows and orphans*
> *and help those in need.*[18]

The Judeans paid little attention to Isaiah's warnings, [6] preferring instead to bask in the glow of their miraculous deliverance from the Assyrians. When representatives came from Babylon to hear the story, Hezekiah warmly received them and gave them a grand tour of the palace and the Temple with all the

---

[16] Isaiah 29:13 (TNIV)

[17] Isaiah 1:11-12 (CEV)

[18] Isaiah 1:15-17 (CEV)

golden treasures each contained. Isaiah told Hezekiah how foolish this was, for it would be the Babylonians who would one day destroy Jerusalem and carry off Hezekiah's descendants. Rather than be horrified at this, Hezekiah took comfort in knowing that such devastation would not come in his lifetime.[19]

Such crass self-centeredness made Isaiah realize how far short Hezekiah fell from God's ideal. Isaiah looked forward to a king who would be everything he had hoped Hezekiah would be:

> *He will delight in obeying the LORD.*
> *He will not judge by appearance*
> *nor make a decision based on hearsay.*
> *He will give justice to the poor*
> *and make fair decisions for the exploited.*
> *The earth will shake at the force of his word,*
> *and one breath from his mouth will destroy the wicked.*[20]

7 Isaiah's hopes were certainly not fulfilled in the next king. After Hezekiah's death, his son, Manasseh, became king at twelve years of age and ruled fifty-five years. Virtually all the reforms that his father had implemented were undone by Manasseh, who rebuilt all the worship shrines throughout the country and even built altars to Baal and Asherah as King Ahab had done in Israel generations earlier. Manasseh desecrated the Temple by worshipping other gods there, sacrificed his son as a burnt offering, practiced sorcery and divination, and consulted mediums and spiritists. Manasseh brought about the death of many innocent people.[21]

God sent prophets to Manasseh and the people of Judah, but they paid little attention to what they said. Then Judah was defeated in battle and Manasseh was taken prisoner. The Babylonians put a hook in the king's nose, bound him with bronze shackles and carried him away. Seeing how this experience humbled Manasseh, God made it possible for him to return to Jerusalem

---

[19] 2 Kings 20:12-19; 2 Chronicles 32:31; Isaiah 39:1-8

[20] Isaiah 11:3-4 (NLT)

[21] 2 Kings 21:1-9; 21:16; 2 Chronicles 33:1-9

and regain his throne. Manasseh's repentance briefly led to minor religious reforms, but the people continued their worship of false gods as before.[22]

Isaiah used the imagery of a vineyard to declare that Judah's destiny would be the same as that of Israel because neither cared for the poor and oppressed:

> *I am the LORD All-Powerful!*
> *Israel is the vineyard,*
> *and Judah is the garden I tended with care.*
> *I had hoped for honesty and for justice,*
> *but dishonesty and cries for mercy*
> *were all I found.*[23]

When Manasseh's reign ended, his son ruled briefly until he was assassinated and Josiah, Manasseh's grandson, became king at eight years of age. Josiah's reign of more than thirty years was peaceful at first because Assyrian power was declining, and neither Egypt nor Babylon was strong enough yet to expand their territories. Freedom from external pressure allowed Josiah to look at what was happening with his own people. He soon realized reforms were desperately needed.[24]

The prophet Zephaniah declared Jerusalem to be filled with those who were oppressive, rebellious and defiled. The leaders were like wild animals, seeking someone to devour. The priests were corrupt, and the prophets were blinded by arrogance.[25]

Using vivid metaphors, Zephaniah described a day of wrath that was coming. This time, Jerusalem would not be spared:

> *I will crush Judah and Jerusalem with my fist*
> *and destroy every last trace of their Baal worship.*
> *I will put an end to all the idolatrous priests,*

---

[22] 2 Chronicles 33:10-17

[23] Isaiah 5:7 (CEV)

[24] 2 Kings 21:19-26; 22:1-2; 2 Chronicles 33:20-25; 34:1-7

[25] Zephaniah 3:1-5

so that even the memory of them will disappear. [26]

That terrible day of the LORD is near.
Swiftly it comes – a day of bitter tears,
a day when even strong men will cry out. [27]

Perhaps it was such warnings by the prophets that led Josiah to carry out religious reforms, beginning with a major restoration of the Temple. While the Temple was being cleaned, one of the king's officials brought news that a copy of the Torah had been discovered there. The king asked to have it read to him, and as he listened to it, he tore his robes in dismay at how far his ancestors had strayed from what the Torah required.[28]

Josiah sent the high priest and other officials to determine what God would have them do. They sought out Huldah, a prophetess who gave them a message from God: "I am going to bring disaster on this place in accordance with everything in the book you have read, but because you have turned to me in faithfulness, it will not happen in your lifetime."[29]

Josiah hoped to avoid the promised disaster, but knew it would not be easy. The Judeans could not expect God to honor their fasting if they were abusing their workers at the same time that they were abstaining from food. The Sabbath rest meant nothing if it led to quarrels and fights between people. God would hear their prayers and accept their worship when they finally began living by righteous standards:

I'll tell you what it really means to worship the LORD.
Remove the chains of prisoners who are chained unjustly.
Free those who are abused!
Share your food with everyone who is hungry;
Share your home with the poor and homeless.

---

[26] Zephaniah 1:4 (NLT)

[27] Zephaniah 1:14 (NLT)

[28] 2 Kings 22:3-11; 2 Chronicles 34:8-21

[29] 2 Kings 22:14-20; 2 Chronicles 34:22-28

Give clothes to those in need...[30]

Josiah determined to do everything possible to change the fate of his people. He called them together and read to them what was written in the book he had found. When the king had finished, he and the people renewed their promise to follow the Torah.[31]

Josiah undertook further reforms by ordering that everything associated with worship of idols and false gods be gathered and completely destroyed. The king's decrees were carried out throughout the kingdom of Judah and even beyond. Worship centers established more than three hundred years earlier by Solomon for his foreign wives and by Jeroboam in the northern cities of Dan and Bethel were destroyed.[32]

Josiah's reforms removed all the priests associated with these worship centers and all mediums and spiritists. The household gods were destroyed as well. Then Josiah commanded that Passover be observed exactly as prescribed in the Torah, something that had not been done even under Hezekiah's reforms.[33]

Despite Josiah's extensive reforms, Judah was too far gone. His reign and reforms lasted thirteen more years until the army of Egypt marched through Judah to join up with Assyria in hopes of defeating the growing power of Babylon. Josiah was killed trying to prevent Egypt from passing through his country.[34]

The ending of Josiah's life roughly coincided with the end of Assyria, as the growing power of Babylon proved too great even for the alliance of Assyria and Egypt. Nineveh was destroyed in 612 BCE and the rest of Assyria in the next few years. The prophet Nahum said the destruction of Assyria would be cause for celebration:

---

[30] Isaiah 58:6-7 (CEV); Jeremiah 3:1

[31] 2 Kings 23:1-3; 2 Chronicles 34:29-32

[32] 2 Kings 23:4-20; 2 Chronicles 34:33

[33] 2 Kings 23:21-27; Joshua 5:10-12; 2 Chronicles 35:1-19

[34] 2 Kings 23:28-30

Your shepherds are asleep, O Assyrian king;
*   your princes lie dead in the dust.*
Your people are scattered across the mountains
*   with no one to gather them together.*
There is no healing for your wound;
*   your injury is fatal.*
All who hear of your destruction
*   will clap their hands for joy.*
Where can anyone be found
*   who has not suffered from your continual cruelty?* [35]

Unfortunately, the demise of Assyria brought only brief respite for Judah. The prophet Habakkuk could see that disaster was on the horizon. Even so, he placed his ultimate hope in the LORD:

Though the fig tree does not bud
*   and there are no grapes on the vines,*
though the olive crop fails
*   and the fields produce no food,*
though there are no sheep in the pen
*   and no cattle in the stalls,*
yet I will rejoice in the LORD,
*   I will be joyful in God my Savior.*[36]

---

[35] Nahum 3:18-19 (NLT)
[36] Habakkuk 3:15-18 (TNIV)

Questions for Reflection/Discussion

1. Micah said God wanted justice, mercy, and humble obedience from the Israelites. To what extent does our society share these values? How different would your life look if you made them a priority?

2. The Assyrians mistakenly thought Hezekiah had rebelled against God by destroying so many worship sites. What actions by believers today might be misunderstood by outsiders?

3. The Assyrians falsely promised the Judeans a land where they would live in peace and prosperity. Are there ways in which people today are offered counterfeit versions of God's blessings and promises? Give an example.

4. God was not impressed with the offerings people brought in worship. What about our offerings today? How do you think God might respond to our worship services?

5. The prophets repeatedly described righteousness as having religious dimensions (not worshipping false gods) and political dimensions (providing justice for the poor). What have you been taught about the meaning of righteousness? How about self-righteousness?

6. Hezekiah was relieved that the coming destruction would not take place in his lifetime. In what ways might future generations have to suffer the consequences of actions we are taking today?

7. Manasseh undid all the reforms Hezekiah had implemented. Why do you think Hezekiah and Manasseh had such radically different values? In what ways are the values of today's young people similar to the values of their parents or grandparents?

CHAPTER 13:
THE FALL OF JERUSALEM

With Assyria's collapse, Egypt and Babylon began to dominate the Mideast. Following Josiah's death, one of his sons, Jehoahaz, served as king for a few months until Egypt let it be known that they preferred Jehoiakim, another of Josiah's sons. Jehoiakim's eleven year reign was characterized by weakness as he was controlled by either the Egyptians or the Babylonians, whichever was more powerful at the moment.[1]

It was during this difficult time that Jeremiah was called to be a prophet. After protesting that he was too young for such a responsibility, Jeremiah was reassured by God that he need not be afraid because God would be with him as long as he was faithful in telling the people what God wanted them to hear.[2]

God gave Jeremiah many messages and told him to have his scribe, Baruch, write them down. The resulting scroll was read to the people and then to the priests. When it was brought to Jehoiakim, the king showed his contempt by burning up the scroll piece by piece as it was read. Jeremiah then had Baruch write another scroll.[3]

1   God told Jeremiah to buy a new linen belt and put it around his waist. Later he told Jeremiah to bury the belt. He dug it up many days later, and found it ruined and useless.

> This is what the LORD says: "These wicked people, who refuse to listen to my words, who follow the stubbornness of their hearts and go after other gods to serve and worship them, will be like this belt – completely useless!"[4]

One day Jeremiah had an interesting encounter with members of the Rekabite clan. They refused Jeremiah's offer of wine, saying

---

[1] 2 Kings 23:36-37; 24:1-7
[2] Jeremiah 1:4-8
[3] Jeremiah 36:1-32
[4] Jeremiah 13:1-11 (TNIV)

their ancestor from generations before told them never to drink wine, build houses, sow seed or plant vineyards, but always to live in tents as nomads. Jeremiah saw the irony: this clan could keep the commands of its ancestor for generations, but the people of Judah could not keep the commands of the LORD for any time at all.[5]

Jeremiah, whose continued warnings of impending calamity went unheeded for most of his life, came to be known as "the weeping prophet." When Nebuchadnezzar defeated the Egyptian forces at Carchemish in 605 BCE, the Babylonians were at the peak of their power. They captured several Philistine cities soon after, and Jehoiakim was given a choice: become a vassal of the Babylonians or see the cities of Judah destroyed.[6]

Jehoiakim became a vassal, but his loyalty to Babylon didn't last long. The very next year, Nebuchadnezzar attempted to invade Egypt, but retreated to Babylon when he was unsuccessful. Jehoiakim thought this sign of weakness offered a chance to break free, but he was mistaken. The Babylonians returned with a mighty army and besieged Jerusalem. Jehoiakim died soon after and his son, Jehoiachin, reigned throughout the siege. When Jehoiachin surrendered, he was taken to Babylon along with most of the prominent people of the city.[7]

Descendants of David had sat on the throne in Jerusalem for more than four hundred years. Jehoiachin was the last to do so.

Shortly after the first group of Jews had been deported from Jerusalem to Babylon, Ezekiel was called to be a prophet. He was to be a watchman who would be accountable for the fate of his people if he failed to relate to them God's warnings.[8]

Although Jeremiah was in Jerusalem and Ezekiel in Babylon, their messages affected people in both places as both prophets

---

[5] Jeremiah 35:1-16

[6] 2 Kings 24:1

[7] 2 Kings 24:9-16; 2 Chronicles 36:5-10; Ezekiel 1:1-3

[8] Ezekiel 3:16-19; 33:1-9

confronted the popular theology of their day and explained what it meant to live in accordance with the Torah.

> **3** | *1. According to popular theology, the Israelites were special because God had given them the Torah.*

Jeremiah said the Jews were not the people of the Torah as they claimed to be because their teachers had distorted the Torah and the people followed the example of their teachers.[9]

God told Ezekiel that Judah was like a useless vine, thrown in the fire, charred at both ends and burned in the middle.

> *If it was not useful for anything when it was whole, how much less can it be made into something useful when the fire has burned it and it is charred?*[10]

> **4** | *2. According to popular theology, the Promised Land had been given by God to the Israelites to be theirs forever.*

Jeremiah argued that the Israelites would be allowed to stay in the Land only if they lived in accordance with the Torah.

> *If you really change your ways and your actions and deal with each other justly, if you do not oppress the alien, the fatherless or the widow and do not shed innocent blood in this place, and if you do not follow other gods to your own harm, then I will let you live in this place, in the land I gave your forefathers for ever and ever.*[11]

Those who remained in Jerusalem following the first deportation believed they were the future of Israel, but Ezekiel told them God would gather the remnant from the countries to which they had been scattered and bring them back to the Promised Land:

> *I will give them an undivided heart and put a new spirit in them; I will remove from them their heart of stone and give them a heart of flesh. Then they will follow my*

---

[9] Jeremiah 8:8-9; 14:11-16
[10] Ezekiel 15:1-8
[11] Jeremiah 7:5-7 (TNIV)

decrees and be careful to keep my laws. They will be my
people, and I will be their God.12

3. According to popular theology, God had promised that
a descendant of David would always reign in Jerusalem.

Jeremiah said God's promise would hold true only if David's
descendants ruled with justice and righteousness:

> *This is what the LORD says: "Be fair-minded and just. Do*
> *what is right! Help those who have been robbed; rescue*
> *them from their oppressors. Quit your evil deeds! Do not*
> *mistreat foreigners, orphans, and widows. Stop murdering*
> *the innocent! If you obey me, there will always be a*
> *descendant of David sitting on the throne here in*
> *Jerusalem."*[13]

Ezekiel said Judah was being judged because its kings, as
descendants of David, should have recognized their role as
shepherds, but failed to do so. Because these "shepherds" cared
only about their own welfare, the sheep would suffer until such a
time as a descendant of David would come as a good shepherd.[14]

4. According to popular theology, God's presence dwelt
within the Temple in Jerusalem.

Jeremiah said the Temple was no guarantee of safety for those
who refused to live in accordance with the Torah:

> *Don't be fooled into thinking that you will never suffer*
> *because the Temple is here. It's a lie! Do you really think*
> *you can steal, murder, commit adultery, lie, and burn*
> *incense to Baal and all those other new gods of yours, and*
> *then come here and stand before me in my Temple and*
> *chant, "We are safe!" – only to go right back to all those*
> *evils again? Don't you yourselves admit that this Temple,*

---

[12] Ezekiel 11:19-20 (TNIV)
[13] Jeremiah 22:3-4 (NLT)
[14] Ezekiel 34:1-24

which bears my name, has become a den of thieves?[15]

Ezekiel was transported to Jerusalem by the Spirit and saw things in the Temple that showed it was no longer the place where God dwelt. Ezekiel saw a statue to the goddess, Asherah, and in a secret chamber of the Temple he saw idols of detestable lions and serpents on the walls, with Israel's leaders burning incense to the images because they believed God had abandoned them. He saw a group of women mourning Tammuz, an ancient Sumerian god. Finally, he saw twenty-five men bowing in prayer toward the Sun god with their backs to the Holy of Holies.[16]

Ezekiel had another vision of the Temple and realized that those who had been left behind had drawn all the wrong conclusions from being spared. They thought they were safe and secure, but Ezekiel told them the worst was yet to come. Ezekiel's vision ended with God abandoning the Temple and returning to his heavenly throne.[17]

In contrast to these beliefs of popular theology, Jeremiah and Ezekiel said God's people had been chosen to live in accordance with two mandates of the Torah:

1. You must worship no god but the LORD, and you must bow to no images or idols under any circumstances.

Jeremiah said Judah was destined to be destroyed because they had repeatedly done something unbelievably foolish:

> *Has any nation ever traded its gods for new ones,*
> *even though they are not gods at all?*
> *Yet my people have exchanged their glorious God*
> *for worthless idols!*
> *For my people have done two evil things:*
> *They have abandoned me – the fountain of living water.*
> *And they have dug for themselves cracked cisterns*

---

[15] Jeremiah 7:4; 7:9-11 (NLT)

[16] Ezekiel 8:1-18

[17] Ezekiel 10:1-22; 11:1-12; 11:22-25

that can hold no water at all![18]

Jeremiah said these "gods that are not gods" cannot speak and cannot walk. He said they even have to be nailed down to keep from falling over. Jeremiah assured the people of Judah they had nothing to fear from such gods – and no reason to look to them for help either.[19]

Ezekiel announced that those who were in Babylon were equally foolish. They may not have made idols with their hands, but they had established them in their hearts.[20]

2. You must live humble lives of integrity characterized by compassion for the poor and powerless

Jeremiah said the people of Judah were overly tolerant of those in their midst who perpetuated injustice.

A hunter traps birds and puts them in a cage,
    but some of you trap humans
    and make them your slaves.
You are evil, and you lie and cheat
    to make yourselves rich.
You are powerful and prosperous, but you refuse
    to help the poor get the justice they deserve.[21]

Ezekiel described how far the people of Judah had fallen:

Your own leaders use their power to murder. None of you honor your parents, and you cheat foreigners, orphans, and widows. You show no respect for my sacred places and treat the Sabbath just like any other day. Some of your own people tell lies, so that others will be put to death. Some of you eat meat sacrificed to idols at local shrines, and others never stop doing vulgar things. Men have sex with their father's wife or with women who are having

---

[18] Jeremiah 2:11; 2:13 (NLT)
[19] Jeremiah 10:2-5
[20] Ezekiel 14:1-6
[21] Jeremiah 5:26-28 (CEV)

their monthly period or with someone else's wife. Some men even sleep with their own daughter-in-law or half sister. Others of you accept money to murder someone. Your own people charge high interest when making a loan to other Israelites, and they get rich by cheating. Worst of all, you have forgotten me, the LORD God.[22]

7 Neither the warnings of Jeremiah nor of Ezekiel made much of an impression on people. Ezekiel's message to the first deportees fell on deaf ears because the people were not prepared to hear that this was only the beginning of their troubles. Ezekiel assured them that his visions and prophecies of future calamities would soon be fulfilled.[23]

Ezekiel said people should not imagine they could live any way they wanted and not be held accountable for it. But God would take no pleasure in the judgment and punishment that would surely come. God wanted people to repent and live.[24]

Unfortunately, what God wanted was not what the people chose. After Jehoiachin had been deposed and taken to Babylon, Zedekiah, a man who was not a descendant of David, was appointed king of Judah by the Babylonians. Rejected by the Jews as an illegitimate king, Zedekiah sought to establish his authority by rebelling against the foreigners who had put him in power. Egypt kept offering to be Judah's ally, and false prophets in Jerusalem were assuring Zedekiah that God would certainly be on his side in seeking independence from Babylon. Heeding their advice and ignoring the words of Jeremiah and Ezekiel, Zedekiah stopped paying tribute to Babylon. It did not take long for the Babylonian army to arrive and besiege Jerusalem.[25]

Zedekiah asked Jeremiah to inquire of the LORD whether they might be delivered. The answer he received was devastating: those who surrender to the Babylonians will live; those who stay

---

[22] Ezekiel 22:6-12 (CEV)

[23] Ezekiel 12:21-28

[24] Ezekiel 18:25-32

[25] 2 Kings 25:3-7; 2 Chronicles 36:11-13; Jeremiah 52:4-5

in the city are sure to die in battle or by famine or plague. The city would be given by God into the hands of the Babylonians and burned to the ground.[26]

Incensed by this message, Zedekiah accused Jeremiah of treason for discouraging the soldiers in Jerusalem. Jeremiah would surely have been executed had not an Egyptian appealed to King Zedekiah on his behalf. This was one of the few occasions when someone came to the aid of this prophet who was regularly treated with scorn. Jeremiah hated the task he had been given, but felt he could neither be silent nor untruthful:

> *You have let me announce*
> *only destruction and death.*
> *Your message has brought me*
> *nothing but insults and trouble.*
> *Sometimes I tell myself not to think about you, LORD,*
> *or even mention your name.*
> *But your message burns in my heart and bones,*
> *and I cannot keep silent.* [27]

The false prophets had no such struggles – they simply told everyone what they wanted to hear and were quite popular because of it. God assured Jeremiah these prophets would be held accountable for the lies and fantasies they said were from the LORD.[28]

The imminent destruction of Jerusalem did not mean the city had no future. Jeremiah was told by God to buy a field from his family's holdings as a sign of better days to come. Those who were soon to be taken from the Land would one day return.[29]

Though this gave hope for the future, in the meantime, the siege continued and the situation grew dire. When the food supplies in Jerusalem were gone, people began to starve. The army became

---

[26] Jeremiah 21:1-10
[27] Jeremiah 20:8-9 (CEV)
[28] Jeremiah 23:25-32
[29] Jeremiah 32:1-15; 32:37-41

too weak to defend the city and the Babylonians broke down its walls. Zedekiah and his army fled, but were soon captured. The last thing Zedekiah saw was the execution of his sons before Nebuzaradan, the commander of the Babylonian army, put out Zedekiah's eyes and took him in shackles to Babylon where he died in prison.[30]

Before leaving Jerusalem, Nebuzaradan set fire to the Temple, the palaces and almost everything else in Jerusalem. His army broke down the walls around the city and carried away into exile most of those who had not died by famine or plague. Only Jeremiah and a few others were left behind.[31]

Jeremiah lamented the destruction of Jerusalem:

Jerusalem, once so full of people,
*   is now deserted.*
She who was once great among the nations
*   now sits alone like a widow.*
Once the queen of all the earth,
*   she is now a slave.*
* She sobs through the night;*
*   tears stream down her cheeks.*[32]

The enemy has plundered her completely,
*   taking every precious thing she owns.*
She has seen foreigners violate her sacred Temple,
*   the place the LORD had forbidden them to enter.*[33]

Your prophets have said so many foolish things,
*   false to the core.*
They did not save you from exile
*   by pointing out your sins.*
Instead, they painted false pictures,

---

[30] 2 Kings 25:1-7; 2 Chronicles 36:11-14; Jeremiah 39:1-7; 52:6-11
[31] 2 Kings 25:8-21; 2 Chronicles 36:15-20; Jeremiah 39:8-10; 52:12-19
[32] Lamentations 1:1-2 (NLT)
[33] Lamentations 1:10 (NLT)

filling you with false hope.[34]

Yet I still dare to hope
when I remember this:
The faithful love of the LORD never ends!
His mercies never cease.
Great is his faithfulness;
his mercies begin afresh each morning.[35]

Restore us, O LORD, and bring us back to you again!
Give us back the joys we once had!
Or have you utterly rejected us?[36]

Though most in Jerusalem saw the victory of the Babylonians as proof of God's abandonment, Jeremiah came to see that Nebuchadnezzar was unknowingly God's servant. All nations would be under Babylon's control for now, but the time would come when Babylon would be overthrown by others.[37]

Jeremiah made this clear in a message sent to the exiles:

When you finish praying, tie the scroll to a rock and throw it in the Euphrates River. Then say, "This is how Babylon will sink when the LORD destroys it. Everyone in the city will die, and it won't have the strength to rise again." [38]

The Babylonians appointed Gedaliah, who was not a descendant of David, to govern those who had been left behind. Some Jews who had fled to other countries returned to join the remnant that had been left in Judah. Among them was Ishmael, a descendant of David who resented Gedaliah being named governor. Ishmael assassinated Gedaliah and fled the country. Those who were left turned to Jeremiah for advice. Should they stay in Judah or seek

---

[34] Lamentations 2:14 (NLT)
[35] Lamentations 3:21-23 (NLT)
[36] Lamentations 5:21-22 (NLT)
[37] Jeremiah 27:1-11
[38] Jeremiah 51:63-64 (CEV)

refuge elsewhere?[39]

Jeremiah said if they stayed in Jerusalem, God would show them compassion, protect them and restore them, but if they fled to Egypt for safety, disaster would surely befall them.[40]

The people refused to accept Jeremiah's message because they were afraid that Jeremiah would hand them over to the Babylonians. They decided to go to Egypt and take Jeremiah with them. Thus some of the Jews returned to Egypt from which God had delivered their ancestors and others were taken in captivity to Babylon from which God had called Abraham.[41]

Jeremiah warned those in Egypt not to continue to worship their idols, but the people refused to listen. They said things had been better when they were worshipping the Queen of Heaven. From what they could see, worshipping the LORD brought them no benefit at all.[42]

Those who had been taken in captivity to Babylon came to see things differently. In the midst of their humiliation and suffering they would make new efforts to live in accordance with the Torah.

---

[39] Jeremiah 40:1-16; 41:1-18; 42:1-3
[40] Jeremiah 42:9-22
[41] Jeremiah 43:1-7
[42] Jeremiah 44:15-18

Questions for Reflection/Discussion

1. God said the people of Judah had become ruined and useless like a linen belt that had been buried. What might a "ruined and useless" church look like today? How might God's evaluation of a church be similar to or different from our own?

2. Jehoiakim's decision to rebel against Babylon turned out far worse than he imagined. What wars have been worse than our leaders imagined? Which ones have been worse than our enemies imagined?

3. The people of Judah felt they were special because God had given them the Torah. What makes you feel you are special? Is your hometown special? Your state? Your country? Your sports teams? Your church? What are the benefits and the dangers of feeling special?

4. The people of Judah felt the Promised Land had been given to them forever. Do we have anything that we believe should belong to our descendants forever? Does a sense of entitlement impact our discussions of immigration? Should it?

5. The House of David felt they should always be in power no matter what. How is this similar to or different from the way our leaders and political parties look at things today?

6. The people in Jerusalem believed they were safe because God's Temple was there. What might give your country a false sense of security? How about your community, church or family?

7. Jeremiah and Ezekiel warned the people about worshipping false idols and ignoring the needs of the poor and powerless. In what ways might these warnings apply to us?

CHAPTER 14:
EXILED IN BABYLON

The first Jews who arrived in Babylon hoped their exile would be brief and they would be allowed to return to Jerusalem. Jeremiah sent a letter telling them to settle in because they were going to be there for a while. They were to do all the normal things – build houses, plant gardens, get married, and raise their children. More than that, they were to pray for the very people who had carried them off into captivity:

> *Seek the peace and prosperity of the city to which I have carried you into exile. Pray for it, because if it prospers, you too will prosper.* [1]

To those who complained about the unfairness of being carried off into exile, Jeremiah responded with questions. Does not a potter have the right to shape a piece of clay in a new way if what he first attempted did not turn out as intended? Should not the LORD have similar freedom in shaping the Jews into what they were designed to be? [2]

1 As the first exiles were joined by those deported after Zedekiah's doomed rebellion, the number of Jews living in Babylon grew to about 25,000. The situation felt hopeless. They had been taken from "the land of milk and honey" to live on the hot plains of Babylon. The last king from the House of David was in prison. The Temple had been ransacked and burned to the ground. Jerusalem, the beautiful "city of Zion" lay in ruins. The LORD had surely abandoned them. It is not surprising they were inconsolable in their grief: [3]

> *Beside the rivers of Babylon, we sat and wept*
> *   as we thought of Jerusalem.*
> *We put away our harps,*
> *   hanging them on the branches of poplar trees.*

---

[1] Jeremiah 29:7 (TNIV)
[2] Jeremiah 18:1-6
[3] Jeremiah 52:28-30

For our captors demanded a song from us.
Our tormentors insisted on a joyful hymn:
"Sing us one of those songs of Jerusalem!"
But how can we sing the songs of the LORD
while in a pagan land? [4]

Many thought those who went into exile were being punished and those who remained in Jerusalem were the hope of the future. Jeremiah said the situation was just the opposite. Those who were living in exile would one day turn to God with all their heart and return to Jerusalem. Those who had not been carried off by the Babylonians would one day flee to Egypt where they would have no end of troubles. [5]

In the midst of their despair, the people heard a message of hope from Jeremiah, the prophet who had earlier spoken such harsh words.

2

For I know the plans I have for you," declares the LORD,
"plans to prosper you and not to harm you, plans to give
you hope and a future." [6]

People drew strength from these words of Jeremiah and from the prophet Isaiah's message.

The LORD is the everlasting God,
The Creator of the ends of the earth.
He gives strength to the weary
and increases the power of the weak.
Even youths grow tired and weary,
and young men stumble and fall;
but those who hope in the LORD
will renew their strength.
They will soar on wings like eagles;
they will run and not grow weary,

---

[4] Psalm 137:1-4 (NLT)
[5] Jeremiah 24:4-10
[6] Jeremiah 29:11 (TNIV)

they will walk and not be faint.[7]

3 The people would need this kind of strength because reminders of oppression were everywhere. In accordance with the way they treated all their captives, the Babylonians sought to show the total authority they had by requiring the Jews to conform by changing their names, diets, language, clothing and religion. Those who resisted such changes were considered dangerous.

King Nebuchadnezzar decided the brightest and best of the young Jews should enter his service. To "cleanse" them from the remnants of their "Jewishness" and make them fit to serve the king, these young men would be given new names and taught a new language. They would also have to follow a new diet.[8]

Among those chosen were Daniel, Hananiah, Mishael and Azariah. In accordance with the king's decree, they were given new names: Belteshazzar (which means "protect the king"), Shadrach, Meshach and Abednego. They accepted their new names and responsibilities, but resolved not to defile themselves by eating royal food that would include meat declared by the Torah to be unclean. Daniel proposed a test: give the Jewish trainees nothing but vegetables for ten days and see how they compared to the young men living on royal diets. A vegetarian diet would not only be acceptable under the restrictions of the Torah, but would also be more appropriate than rich food and drink for those grieving life in exile.[9]

At the end of the ten days, the official concluded that Daniel and his friends could eat as they chose because they were in better shape than any of the others. After their three years of training were complete, the king decided that Daniel and his friends were at the top of their class. Not only had they mastered the material they had been given, but Daniel had also showed an ability to understand visions and dreams. Throughout the years of exile,

---

[7] Isaiah 40:28-31 (TNIV)
[8] Daniel 1:1-5
[9] Daniel 1:6-14

Daniel remained a servant of the king.[10]

At one point, King Nebuchadnezzar was troubled by a series of dreams. He called together his wise men and astrologers, asking them to tell him what the dreams meant without him telling them what the dreams were. The king's advisers were shocked, saying such a request had never been made in history. The king persisted because he said that was the only way he could know he was being told the truth. When the wise men and astrologers had nothing to say, the king ordered their execution.[11]

Daniel heard what the king had done and asked permission to interpret the dreams. Daniel and his friends prayed, and during the night Daniel received a vision from God. The next morning the king asked Daniel if he could interpret his dream. Daniel replied that only God could reveal such mysteries. Then Daniel described an enormous statue the king had seen in his dream.[12]

Daniel explained that the statue's head of gold was the kingdom of Babylon under the rule of Nebuchadnezzar. After Babylon's time had ended, an inferior kingdom would arise and then two more kingdoms. The last of these would be a divided one, partly as strong as iron and partly as brittle as clay. The rock that shattered the statue from head to toe would be a kingdom set up by the God of heaven.[13]

The king was awe-struck at Daniel's words and acknowledged that Daniel must indeed serve the God of gods. To show his appreciation, the king appointed Daniel and his friends to high positions in the royal court.[14]

Things went well for a while, but it was not long before the king made an enormous image of gold and commanded everyone to bow down before it whenever they heard the royal

4

---

[10] Daniel 1:15-21
[11] Daniel 2:1-13
[12] Daniel 2:14-35
[13] Daniel 2:36-45
[14] Daniel 2:46-49

musicians play. When the king learned that some Jewish officials who were Daniel's friends refused to bow down, he was furious. The king ordered them to defend themselves or be thrown into a fiery furnace. Shadrach, Meshach, and Abednego told the king they had no need to defend themselves. Regardless of what the king did, they were in the LORD's hands. Either God would save them from the fiery furnace or they would become martyrs to their faith. They were prepared to accept whichever fate awaited them.[15]

The king had them thrown into the furnace, but was shocked to see four men walking around in the fire, with the fourth one looking like a heavenly being. Amazed both by their faith and God's power, the king ordered Daniel's friends to come out of the furnace. He even gave them promotions.[16]

The example of Daniel and his friends must have been a great encouragement to other exiles because it showed that God had not totally abandoned them. This was reinforced by the prophets.

5   Isaiah said that Israel was not to forget its heritage, but neither was it to yearn for the past so much that it blinded them to what God was now doing.

> *I am the LORD, who opened a way through the waters,*
>   *making a dry path through the sea.*
> *I called forth the mighty army of Egypt*
>   *with all its chariots and horses.*
> *I drew them beneath the waves, and they drowned,*
>   *their lives snuffed out like a smoldering candlewick.*
>
> *But forget all that—*
>   *it is nothing compared to what I am going to do.*[17]

Isaiah's message gave the people new hope that perhaps they had not been rejected and abandoned.

---

[15] Daniel 3:1-18

[16] Daniel 3:25-30

[17] Isaiah 43:16-18 (NLT)

Can a mother forget her nursing child?
  Can she feel no love for the child she has borne?
But even if that were possible,
  I would not forget you!
See, I have written your name on the palms of my hands.
  Always in my mind
  is a picture of Jerusalem's walls in ruins.[18]

Through Isaiah, the people understood that their suffering was not intended to destroy them, but to purify them. The punishment they received for their sins and the sins of their ancestors was intended by God to be limited and purposeful. This was a drastic action, but one that God thought was necessary because the righteousness with which the people of Judah sought to clothe themselves was in truth nothing more than filthy rags.[19]

Those in exile didn't describe what had happened to them as being part of some great conflict between good and evil, between God and Satan. Rather they saw what happened to them being a direct result of their rebellion against God.[20]

Though defeated as a nation, the people of Judah were assured that this was not a triumph of the Babylonian gods. Such gods were nothing more than idols made by human hands. Anyone who believed such gods could save them was being foolish.[21]

The fact that the LORD was God over all the nations would soon be evident because God was anointing Cyrus, leader of the Persians, to deliver the Jews from their exile in Babylon. What would make this truly remarkable was that Cyrus would not even acknowledge the LORD's existence while being used in this way to carry out God's plan.[22]

Though Babylon had earlier been used by God to humble the

---

[18] Isaiah 49:15-16 (NLT)

[19] Isaiah 64:4-7

[20] Isaiah 42:23-25

[21] Isaiah 44:13-18

[22] Isaiah 45:1-5

people of Judah, their own destruction was assured. No longer would Babylon be called the queen of kingdoms. Because the Babylonians had treated cruelly those they defeated, showing no mercy even to those who were too old to resist, a catastrophe would soon come upon the Babylonian Empire.[23]

The end came on a night when King Belshazzar of Babylon was giving a banquet at which he used the gold goblets that his father had brought from the Temple in Jerusalem. As the king and his nobles drank from the goblets and honored false gods, a finger of a human hand appeared and wrote a message on the wall.[24]

Terrified by what he had seen, the king summoned his magicians and astrologers to learn what the words meant. But none of them had any idea. The queen then called for Daniel to be brought in, explaining that in earlier days he had astounded everyone with his ability to solve difficult problems.[25]

When Daniel appeared, the king offered him great wealth and honor if he could explain what the writing meant. Daniel refused the king's offered gifts, but told him the meaning of MENE, MENE, TEKEL, PARSIN:

> *God has numbered the days of your kingdom and has brought it to an end. He has weighed you on his balance scales, and you fall short of what it takes to be king. So God has divided your kingdom between the Medes and the Persians.*[26]

That very night Darius the Mede entered the city with his army and killed King Balshazzar. The Babylonian empire quickly crumbled. The prophet Isaiah described the humiliation of the king of Babylon in terms that would later be applied to Satan:

> *The world of the dead eagerly waits for you.*
> *With great excitement, the spirits of ancient rulers*

---

[23] Isaiah 47:5-11

[24] Daniel 5:1-5

[25] Daniel 5:6-12

[26] Daniel 5:26-28 (CEV)

hear about your coming.
Each one of them will say,
   "Now you are just as weak as any of us!
   Your pride and your music have ended here
     in the world of the dead.
   Worms are your blanket, maggots are your bed."
You, the bright morning star,
    have fallen from the sky!
You brought down other nations;
    now you are brought down. [27]

The new king set up a system of seventy local governors and three regional supervisors to rule on his behalf. When the king let it be known that Daniel was to oversee the entire system, many of the governors and supervisors were upset that a Jew should be chosen for such an honor. They conspired against Daniel by encouraging the king to decree that anyone who prayed to any god other than the king should be put to death.[28]

Daniel was determined not to allow such a decree to change the faith by which he had lived his life. Each day he prayed three times by an open window in his house where all who passed by could hear. When this was brought to the king's attention, he had no option but to order Daniel's death. Daniel was thrown into a den of lions and left there overnight. When the king came the next morning, he could see that Daniel was standing in the midst of the lions unharmed. Deciding that he had been misled by his advisors, the king ordered them to take Daniel's place in the lions' den, and they soon met their fate.[29]

The overthrow of the Babylonians by the Medes and Persians gave new hope to the Jews. Ezekiel had a vision in which God brought him to a valley full of bones and told him to speak words of life to them. As Ezekiel did so, the bones began to rattle and join together. Soon the bones were whole and covered

---

[27] Isaiah 14:9-12 (CEV)
[28] Daniel 6:1-9
[29] Daniel 6:10-24

with muscle and flesh. God told Ezekiel to speak again and the breath of life came into the bodies and they stood up on their feet as a mighty army.[30]

Then God told the prophet what this meant:

> *Ezekiel, the people of Israel are like dead bones. They complain that they are dried up and that they have no hope for the future. So tell them, "I, the LORD God, promise to open your graves and set you free. I will bring you back to Israel, and when that happens, you will realize that I am the LORD.*[31]

This was consistent with what Isaiah had said:

> *"For a brief moment I abandoned you,*
> *but with great compassion I will take you back.*
> *In a burst of anger I turned my face away for a little while.*
> *But with everlasting love*
> *I will have compassion on you,"*
> *says the LORD, your Redeemer.*[32]

Now that Babylon's power had been broken, the Jews were convinced their years in exile would soon come to an end. "Weeping may last through the night, but joy comes with the morning."[33]

> *In Ramah a voice is heard, crying and weeping loudly.*
> *Rachel mourns for her children*
> *and refuses to be comforted, because they are dead.*
> *But I, the LORD, say to dry your tears.*
> *Someday your children will come home*
> *from the enemy's land.*
> *Then all you have done for them will be greatly rewarded.*
> *So don't lose hope.*

---

[30] Ezekiel 37:1-10
[31] Ezekiel 37:11-13 (CEV)
[32] Isaiah 54:7-8 (NLT)
[33] Psalm 30:5 (NLT)

I, the LORD, have spoken. [34]

---

[34] Jeremiah 31:15-17 (CEV)

Questions for Reflection/Discussion

1. In exile, the Jews were inconsolable in their grief because they realized they had lost everything they held dear. What losses would your country have to sustain for you to feel such despair?

2. Jeremiah, who often spoke harsh words from God, brought a message of hope to those in exile. Have you heard a message of hope at a particularly low point in your life? What happened afterward?

3. The Jews were required by their captors to give up their names, diets, language, clothing, and religion. If you were imprisoned in a foreign land under similar constraints, to what extent would you comply with or fight against such changes?

4. Daniel's friends refused to obey the king's decree and accepted the consequences of their decision. How are their actions similar to or different from those of civil rights protestors, anti-abortion protestors, anti-war protestors, or strikers who refuse a court order to return to work?

5. God's people were told to remember the past without letting it limit their future. To what extent does yearning for the past limit openness to the future for you? For your family? For your church? For your country?

CHAPTER 15:
RESTORATION

When the Medes and Persians conquered Babylon in 539 BCE, they put an end to a harsh rule that had oppressed the Mideast for seventy years. King Cyrus, seeking a more "enlightened" reign, decided to return captured peoples and their sacred objects to the cities from which they had come. This meant that the Jews could return to their homeland and build a temple there for worship of the LORD.[1]

Jeremiah had said the return from exile in Babylon would be an event even greater than the exodus from Egypt.

> *"But the time is coming," says the LORD, "when people who are taking an oath will no longer say, 'As surely as the LORD lives, who rescued the people of Israel from the land of Egypt.' Instead, they will say, 'As surely as the LORD lives, who brought the people of Israel back to their own land from the land of the north and from all the countries to which he had exiled them.' "* [2]

Unlike Pharaoh, Cyrus did not need devastating plagues to convince him to let the people of God leave his country. He told them they were free to go home, and even told them to take with them the sacred treasures plundered from the Temple.[3]

As they left, the words of Isaiah encouraged them greatly.

> *Leave the city of Babylon!*
> *Don't touch anything filthy. Wash yourselves.*
> *Be ready to carry back everything sacred*
> *that belongs to the LORD.*
> *You won't need to run. No one is chasing you.*
> *The LORD God of Israel*

---

[1] Ezra 1:1-4
[2] Jeremiah 16:14-15; 23:7-8 (NLT)
[3] Ezra 1:6-8

will lead and protect you from enemy attacks. [4]

Although some Jews decided to stay in Babylon, more than 42,000 gladly made preparations for the long journey to their ancestral home. In addition to people from the tribes of Judah and Levi, some from Benjamin, Manasseh and Ephraim returned to Jerusalem as well. [5]

| 1 | This was in accordance with God's promise to give the Israelites a new beginning:

For I will take you out of the nations; I will gather you from all the countries and bring you back into your own land. I will sprinkle clean water on you, and you will be clean; I will cleanse you from all your impurities and from all your idols. I will give you a new heart and put a new spirit in you; I will remove from you your heart of stone and give you a heart of flesh. [6]

As soon as the people had reached their destination, they celebrated their return with burnt offerings and made plans for construction of the Temple. People watched the foundation being laid with mixed reactions. They rejoiced at the idea of a new Temple, but they knew this one would never share the splendor of the one built by Solomon. [7]

| 2 | Those who had repopulated Samaria under the Assyrians two centuries before now offered to help the Jews build the new Temple. The Samaritans said they would like to be part of the project because they had been worshipping the LORD ever since they had come to Samaria. But the Jews rejected their offer, saying this Temple would belong only to God's chosen people, the descendants of Abraham, Isaac and Jacob. Not surprisingly, such a rejection angered the Samaritans who now

---

[4] Isaiah 52:11-12 (CEV)
[5] 1 Chronicles 9:1-44; Ezra 1:5; 2:1-67
[6] Ezekiel 36:24-26 (TNIV)
[7] Ezra 3:10-13

began looking for ways to hinder the Temple's construction.[8]

Opposition by the Samaritans was not the only factor
delaying construction of the Temple. After the initial
[3]
enthusiasm of laying the foundation had dissipated, many of the
Jews turned their attention to building their own houses and
tending their fields. The prophet Haggai confronted this situation
by asking a question: Was it right for them to live in beautiful
houses while the house of God was in ruins?[9]

Haggai reminded the people that although they were once again
living in the Promised Land, things were not going well.

> *Look at what's happening to you! You have planted much
> but harvest little. You eat but are not satisfied. You drink
> but are still thirsty. You put on clothes but cannot keep
> warm. Your wages disappear as though you were putting
> them in pockets filled with holes!*[10]

Chastised by Haggai, the people decided it was time to move
ahead with the Temple. When the Samaritans discovered that
construction had started again, they sent a letter to King Darius
of Persia asking him to halt this unauthorized, seditious project.
Darius searched the archives and discovered what Cyrus had
authorized. Darius reinstated the original decree, going so far as
to tell Jerusalem's regional governor to provide whatever funds
were needed for the construction. This was not what the
Samaritans wanted to hear, especially when Darius added that
anyone obstructing the Jews was to be executed.[11]

With the affirmation of King Darius and the encouragement of
the prophets Haggai and Zechariah, the Temple was completed
and dedicated in 516 BCE. Soon after, the Passover was
celebrated and the regular offering of burnt sacrifices resumed.[12]

---

[8] Ezra 4:1-5
[9] Haggai 1:1-4
[10] Haggai 1:5-6 (NLT)
[11] Ezra 5:1-17; 6:1-12; Zechariah 3:1-7; 4:6-10
[12] Ezra 6:15-22

When a new Persian king, Artaxerxes, came into power, the Samaritans wrote him a letter accusing the Jews of rebuilding the walls of Jerusalem in preparation for a rebellion against the Persian Empire. The king searched his records and discovered that the Jews indeed had a history of rebelling against those who conquered them. He issued an order for all construction in Jerusalem to cease immediately.[13]

Nearly 60 years later, in about 458 BCE, a second group of about 1,500 men plus their families returned to Jerusalem from Babylon with a decree from King Artaxerxes of Persia "to inquire about Judah and Jerusalem with regard to the Law of your God." The leader of this group, Ezra, was a scholar whose life had three priorities: to study the Torah, to live the Torah and to teach the Torah.[14]

Soon after Ezra arrived in Jerusalem, he was forced to confront the extensive intermarriage that had taken place between Jews and Gentiles in clear violation of the Torah. Two things made this particularly bad: 1) the women involved were descendants of the very nations that were to have been driven out of the Promised Land under Joshua; and 2) it was the leaders of the Jewish community who were most guilty of such intermarriage. Ezra was appalled when he learned the extent of the problem. [15]

4   Ezra determined that a commission should be established to investigate each case. Within two months the commission had completed its work and announced the results: 110 marriages would be dissolved, a number representing about one half of one percent of the Jewish community.[16]

Several years later, news of Jerusalem was brought to Nehemiah, a Jewish cupbearer to the king in Babylon. Although the Temple had been rebuilt, the walls of Jerusalem had not been, and the people lived in fear of their neighbors. When Nehemiah heard

---

[13] Ezra 4:6-24
[14] Ezra 7:1-28; 8:1-14
[15] Ezra 9:1-15
[16] Ezra 10:1-44

this, he wept and fasted, praying for success in what he decided to ask the king.[17]

The king noticed his cupbearer's sadness and asked what was wrong. Nehemiah replied, "How can I not be sad when the city of my ancestors lies in ruin?" The king, who had stopped the rebuilding of Jerusalem several years earlier, now offered to help by sending Nehemiah to Jerusalem with a military escort and letters authorizing him to use whatever lumber he needed to build strong gates for the city.[18]

Nehemiah arrived in Jerusalem and spent several days inspecting the damage done to the walls and gates. When he had all the information he needed, Nehemiah called together the city officials and said, "Come, let us rebuild the wall of Jerusalem and we will no longer be in disgrace." They were in full agreement.[19]

Not everyone was pleased that Jerusalem was being rebuilt. The rulers of Samaria and Ammon were troubled when they saw the letters of authorization from King Artaxerxes. They mocked and ridiculed Nehemiah for what he was doing, accusing him of rebelling against the king he claimed to serve. Nehemiah replied that God would give success to the Jews; Samaritans and Ammonites had no claim on Jerusalem.[20]

In spite of such opposition, many Jews offered their services and work began. Several of the city's ten gates needed to be completely rebuilt, as did the northern wall and much of the eastern wall. Although the steep slopes made much of this work incredibly demanding, the large number of workers allowed steady progress. The Ammonites and Samaritans decided they had to attack the city before it was fully fortified, but Nehemiah was prepared: he kept one half of his work force fully armed and

---

[17] Nehemiah 1:1-11
[18] Nehemiah 2:1-8
[19] Nehemiah 2:11-18
[20] Nehemiah 2:9-10; 2:19-20; 4:1-3

standing guard while the other half worked.[21]

Nehemiah was beset by more than these external threats: tensions between the rich and poor threatened to tear the Jewish community apart. Some were forced to pledge their land as they borrowed money to buy grain and pay taxes. Others had no land and could only pledge their children to those who were lending money. What made matters worse was the high rate of interest being charged.[22]

5 Nehemiah was incensed when he learned that people were losing their land or having their children sold into slavery in order to pay off their debts. He said it was not right that some in the community should profit from the misery of others. He demanded that no interest be charged and that penalties for people unable to pay their debts be suspended. The whole assembly said, "Amen," and praised God.[23]

Nehemiah was also concerned to set an example of personal integrity. Throughout his twelve years as governor, he paid for his own expenses and for the entertaining of others out of his own funds rather than using funds at his discretion from the government treasury.[24]

When the walls were finally completed and all that remained was completion of the gates, Nehemiah's enemies made yet another attempt to foil his efforts by sending a report to Babylon that Nehemiah was planning on having himself proclaimed king of Judah as soon as Jerusalem was fully fortified. Nehemiah remained firm in his resolve because he was convinced that unfounded lies could not bring him down as long as he was trusting God.[25]

In less than two months, the walls were repaired and rebuilt. This

---

[21] Nehemiah 4:6-23

[22] Nehemiah 5:1-5

[23] Nehemiah 5:6-13

[24] Nehemiah 5:14-19

[25] Nehemiah 6:1-9

discouraged all of Nehemiah's enemies, who realized they had failed to retain control over Jerusalem even though they had many families in Jerusalem who were connected to them through marriage. These "spies" told Nehemiah's enemies everything.[26]

Now that Jerusalem was a safe and secure city, the time had come to renew the covenant and repopulate the city. Ezra, a priest who specialized in study of the Torah, was invited to come and read the Torah to all who were old enough to understand it. He read for six hours in the square by the Water Gate and the people listened attentively, weeping as they realized how far they had departed from what God had intended.[27]

Nehemiah and Ezra said to the people, "This day is holy to the LORD your God. Do not mourn or weep. For the joy of the LORD is your strength." The people went to their homes to eat and drink and share with others in celebration for the new beginning God had granted them.[28]

The next day, the heads of all the families gathered around Ezra to be instructed in the Torah. They learned about the Festival of Booths and celebrated it for seven days as prescribed. Day after day they met to study the Torah, and soon decided they must confess their sins and the sins of their ancestors:[29]

| 6 |

You have always been fair when you punished us for our sins. Our kings, leaders, and priests have never obeyed your commands or heeded your warnings.[30]

Now we are slaves in this fruitful land you gave to our ancestors. Its plentiful harvest is taken by kings you placed over us because of our sins. Our suffering is

---

[26] Nehemiah 6:16-19

[27] Nehemiah 7:4-5; 8:1-8

[28] Nehemiah 8:9-12

[29] Nehemiah 8:13-18; 9:1-4

[30] Nehemiah 9:33-34 (CEV)

unbearable, because they do as they wish to us and our livestock. [31]

This prayer for grace and deliverance was followed by a binding agreement entered into by the leaders, Levites, and priests on behalf of the people. Everyone bound themselves with a curse and an oath to follow the Torah given through Moses and to obey carefully all the commands, regulations and decrees of the LORD.[32]

Now that Jerusalem was secure and the covenant renewed, the walls were rededicated and the city was repopulated. Seventy years had passed from the destruction of Jerusalem to the rebuilding of the Temple in 515 BCE and another seventy years before Jerusalem's walls were rebuilt in 445 BCE. Lots were cast and ten per cent of the Jews living in Judah moved into Jerusalem and settled there.[33]

7 Nehemiah remained in Jerusalem for twelve years before returning to his position with the Persian king in Babylon. Several years later Nehemiah asked to return to Jerusalem and was granted permission to do so. To his dismay, he discovered that much of the reforms instituted under his leadership had already been forgotten.[34]

- The high priest had cleared out one of the Temple storerooms and had allowed one of Israel's enemies to live in it;

- Tithes had not been collected for support of the Temple, and the Levites and musicians had gone back to work their own fields because they had not been paid for their Temple duties;

- Jews were harvesting their crops on the Sabbath and bringing them into Jerusalem to sell; and,

---

[31] Nehemiah 9:36-37 (CEV)

[32] Nehemiah 9:38; 10:1-39

[33] Nehemiah 11:1-4; 12:27-47

[34] Nehemiah 13:6-7

- Intermarriage with foreigners had resumed to such an extent that even one of the high priest's sons had become the son-in-law of one of Israel's main enemies.[35]

Nehemiah instituted new reforms, including the collection of tithes, the dissolution of marriages to foreigners and the shutting of Jerusalem's gates on the Sabbath to prevent commerce from taking place on that day.[36]

Now that Jerusalem and the Temple had been rebuilt, reforms implemented, and the covenant renewed, everything looked good except for one thing: the people were not free. There was no one from the house of David on the throne in Jerusalem because there was no throne there. The prophet Malachi captured the malaise of the people by confronting them with their hypocrisy and disobedience.

- How have you shown contempt for God's name? *By lighting useless fires on God's altar to offer blind, lame or diseased animals as sacrifices.*[37]

- How have you desecrated God's Temple? *By coming to worship when you have been unfaithful to your wives and chased after immoral women.*[38]

- How have you wearied God? *By saying the God of justice no longer cares what is happening.*[39]

- How have you robbed God? *By not giving your tithes and offerings.*[40]

- How have you spoken arrogantly against God? *By*

---

[35] Nehemiah 13:4-29
[36] Nehemiah 13:8-31
[37] Malachi 1:6-14
[38] Malachi 2:10-16
[39] Malachi 2:17
[40] Malachi 3:8-12

saying there is nothing to gain by serving God.[41]

Malachi was told by God that a day of judgment was coming for all who served false gods or lived false lives.

> *I'm now on my way to judge you. And I will quickly condemn all who practice witchcraft or cheat in marriage or tell lies in court or rob workers of their pay or mistreat widows and orphans or steal the property of foreigners or refuse to respect me.*[42]

But for those who are faithful, the Day of Judgment will include deliverance from evil and the culmination of life as God intended it from the beginning.

> *But for you that honor my name, victory will shine like the sun with healing in its rays, and you will jump around like calves at play. When I come to bring justice, you will trample those who are evil, as though they were ashes under your feet.*[43]

God's final message to Malachi described what would happen as the Day of Judgment drew near.

> *See, I will send you the prophet Elijah before that great and dreadful day of the LORD comes. He will turn the hearts of the fathers to their children, and the hearts of the children to their fathers; or else I will come and strike the land with total destruction."*[44]

---

[41] Malachi 3:13-15
[42] Malachi 3:5 (CEV)
[43] Malachi 4:2-3 (CEV)
[44] Malachi 4:5-6 (TNIV)

Questions for Reflection/Discussion

1. The new beginning for God's people was made possible because God took away their heart of stone and gave them a heart of flesh. What kind of person would you describe as being hard-hearted today?

2. The Jews rejected offers of help because they believed the Samaritans were not part of God's chosen people. In what contexts might the phrase "not one of us" be used to exclude people today?

3. Haggai criticized his fellow Jews for being concerned about their own houses much more than about the house of God. How do we find a balance between providing things for our families and supporting God's mission and the church's ministry?

4. Mixed marriages were having a major negative impact on the Jews and yet less than 1% of the people had married outside the faith. What are some contemporary situations in which small numbers of people might have a large negative impact on society?

5. Nehemiah was upset that some were getting rich by charging excessive rates of interest to those who could least afford it. How is this similar to or different from payday loans, credit card fees and mortgage rates today?

6. At Ezra's urging, the Jews confessed their sins and the sins of their ancestors. How would you feel if someone told you to apologize for the sins of slavery and segregation? Would your feelings be different if you knew your ancestors actually owned slaves, had been members of the Ku Klux Klan, or had attended a racial lynching?

7. After a few years, the reforms Nehemiah instituted were forgotten. What examples of more recent reform have failed to last? Why is it so difficult to bring about real change?

EPILOGUE:
A STORY IN SEARCH OF AN ENDING

For a century following the time of Malachi and the end of the Old Testament, not much changed for the Jews. They continued to be ruled by the Persian Empire until Alexander the Great conquered much of the known world in 332 BCE. Even this major event initially seemed to change little for the Jews. Wasn't Alexander just another powerful foreign ruler who wanted them to worship false gods?

After less than a decade as emperor, Alexander died without an heir and the empire was divided among his generals. Ptolemy was given an area that included Egypt, and Seleucus was given Babylonia (Syria). Both leaders soon had themselves proclaimed king and sought to expand the area they ruled. The land of the Jews served as a buffer zone between these two powerful kingdoms. For more than a century, the Jews were ruled either by the Ptolemies or the Seleucids, depending on which was more powerful at the time.

Although the Greek empire was fractured in its rule, it was united in its culture. As Greek became the universal language, Greek culture and philosophy spread as well. One aspect of Greek thought – an emphasis on the immortality of the soul – led some Jews to focus on life after death rather than on life in this world. Other Jews remained faithful to the belief that one day their exile in this present age with its godless rulers would end, and an age to come would bring with it the reign of God in a restored and renewed creation.

The Hebrew Scriptures were translated into Greek during this period in order to make them more accessible to Jews who now understood Aramaic and Greek, but no longer understood Hebrew. This Greek version of the scriptures was called the Septuagint because of the tradition that seventy scholars had worked on it. Many of the New Testament's quotes are from this Greek translation rather than from the Hebrew originals.

In 198 BCE, the Ptolemies finally relinquished all control of the Jewish territories to the Seleucids, who were being led at that time by Antiochus III (aka *Antiochus the Great*). It appeared that the Seleucids might gain supremacy throughout the ancient world until they were defeated by the Roman army at the battle of Thermopylae.

Antiochus IV (aka *Antiochus Epiphanes*) sought to expand the area of his rule just as his father had. Rather than expanding into Greece, however, Antiochus IV decided to add Egypt to the area he oversaw. Rome sent a message that an attack on Egypt would be considered a declaration of war against Rome, and Antiochus IV withdrew rather than risk defeat.

Soon after this humiliation by Rome, Antiochus learned that an anti-Greek faction in Jerusalem had rebelled against his rule. His response was swift and brutal. First he ordered the execution or enslavement of the rebels. Next he declared circumcision, sacrifices and anything else connected with the Jewish religion to be illegal. Finally, he entered Jerusalem on December 25, 167 BCE and did all he could to profane the Temple – going so far as to enter the Holy of Holies and set up an altar there on which pigs could be sacrificed in worship of the Greek god Zeus.

To the Jews, this outrageous action by Antiochus Epiphanes was the culmination of what had been happening for years. For instance, Antiochus had earlier constructed a gymnasium in which men could exercise and compete. Because Greek games were conducted in the nude, the Jews were scandalized that such a thing should happen in their midst.

Jewish outrage at all that Antiochus Epiphanes had done led to a revolt led by Judas Maccabeus. By resorting to guerilla tactics, the rebels were actually able to gain temporary control over Jerusalem. They built a new altar to replace the desecrated one and rededicated the Temple in 164 BCE. This event has been remembered ever since in the celebration of Hanukkah.

This period in which the Jews were under the control of foreign empires from the Babylonian exile to the Maccabean revolt was described in dreams and visions found in the book of Daniel, and in other books that are listed as the Apocrypha in some versions of the Bible.

Antiochus sent a large army to crush those who had engineered the revolt, but his death led to the army being recalled before ever reaching Judea. Civil war broke out in Syria and the Seleucid dynasty quickly deteriorated. The Maccabean revolt continued to spread, and in 143 BCE the king of Syria granted Judea its independence. This marked the beginning of the Hasmonean regime, a Jewish dynasty that would rule Judea for more than a century.

Now that the Jews were once again an independent nation in control of their own destiny, many concluded that their years of exile had finally come to an end. This was particularly true of the Sadducees, a political party that supported the Hasmoneans.

Another political party, the Pharisees, disagreed. One objection they raised was that the Hasmoneans were not anointed rulers who were descendants of David. Another objection was that the Hasmonean kings also served in the role of high priest even though they were neither properly anointed nor descendants of Aaron. Their final objection was that combining the position of priest and king was not at all in accordance with the Torah.

The Hasmonean rule of Judea continued until Rome began its transition from a republic to an empire. The Roman occupation of Judea began in 63 BCE with Pompey, leader of the Roman army, brazenly entering the Holy of Holies in the Jerusalem Temple just as Antiochus had done a century before. This time, however, there was no Judas Maccabeus to lead a rebellion against the infidel who committed such an outrage.

The Romans extended Pax Romana (Peace of Rome) to every area they conquered. This made it possible for trade and travel to thrive, but such prosperity came at a high price: heavy taxes and brutal suppression of dissent. Roman religion was established throughout the empire, and Judea soon began to be filled with Roman temples, shrines, and altars. Sacred prostitution and the sale of meat that had been dedicated to idols became common. Jews were allowed to practice their own religion, but only if they offered sacrifices to the LORD God on the emperor's behalf. Roman ideas and practices offended those who adhered to the Torah.

At first the Romans allowed the Hasmoneans to rule Judea, but in 43 BCE, Herod the Great was declared by Rome to be the King of the Jews. Herod ruled for nearly forty years, dying about two years after the birth of Jesus. He took many steps to encourage the Jews to accept him as their legitimate king, but even rebuilding the Temple in Jerusalem and marrying the daughter of one of the Hasmoneans was not enough. Herod was an Idumean whose ancestors were descended from Esau rather Jacob. Because the Idumeans had been forcibly converted to Judaism a century earlier, most Jews did not consider him to be one of them.

Four hundred years of being ruled by Persians, Greeks and Romans reinforced the idea for most Jews that they were still living in exile as punishment from God. They wondered if their sins and the sins of their ancestors would ever be forgiven. How would the story that had begun with Abraham, Isaac, and Jacob come to an end? Different groups began to follow paths they hoped would bring the end they desired.

Some followed the path of accommodation. The **Sadducees** had given up hope that God would act in some miraculous way to deliver them, but they saw ways in which they could save themselves through working with the Romans or whoever else was in power. The Sadducees followed the Torah, but only when it addressed specific situations. They saw no validity in the oral traditions and interpretations of the Torah that were so important to the Pharisees. One of the main ways the Sadducees exercised their power was through the appointment of Temple priests, including the Chief Priest. Priests were not chosen because they were descendants of Aaron or for any special calling they had from God, but simply because they were willing to pay the highest price for the right to collect Temple taxes.

Some followed the path of revolution. The **Zealots** claimed no special religious authority and had no political power or influence. They were simply outraged at how the Romans treated the Jews, and were determined to overthrow their pagan oppressors as had happened more than a century earlier in the Maccabean revolt. Their goal was to see a renewed Jewish state with a descendant of David on the throne. The Zealots began their rebellion during the time of Herod with isolated attacks on the Romans. A generation after the time of Jesus, Zealots led a full-scale revolt that was brutally crushed by Roman forces. The Temple was destroyed at that time and never rebuilt.

Some followed a path of purity. The **Pharisees** were committed to the purity that would come through scrupulous obedience to the Torah and to the interpretations of it that had been handed down by oral tradition over the centuries. Because they believed national purity was essential in order for God to act on their behalf, the Pharisees sought to use what little influence they had on those who were in positions of power and authority. The Pharisees despised anyone who failed to obey God's commands, believing that such disobedience was what perpetuated God's punishment and the people's exile.

Some followed a path of separation. The **Essenes** were also devoted to the purity that could only come from obedience to the Torah, but they were even more exclusive than the Pharisees. The Essenes rejected the Temple and the system of sacrifices, arguing that the priests who controlled them were corrupt. In fact, the Essenes saw themselves as *Sons of Light* and all others – Jews and Gentiles alike – as *Sons of Darkness*. The Essenes believed that God was already at work in and through them. They were convinced it would not be long before God would raise up an anointed leader – a Messiah – to deliver true Israel from its pagan rulers and its apostate priests.

It was into this historical context that Jesus was born as the Word who would bring light and order into the darkness and chaos of his world. Jesus would demonstrate through his life, death and resurrection that the next chapter of the story that had begun with Abraham, Isaac, and Jacob would be filled with unexpected twists and turns – and with incredibly good news.

Timeline BCE
(Before Christian Era or Before Common Era)

BCE	Chapter 1: In the Beginning
	Creation
	Adam and Eve
	Noah and the Flood

BCE	Chapter 2: Abraham, Isaac and Jacob
2085	Call of Abram/Abraham
2072	Birth of Ishmael
2060	Birth of Isaac
2000	Birth of Jacob/Israel and Esau
1935	Birth of Reuben, Jacob's first son
1895	Birth of Benjamin, Jacob's 12th son
1880	Joseph rises to power in Egypt
1870	Jacob and his family join Joseph in Egypt

BCE	Chapter 3: Exodus from Egypt
1870	Jacob and his family join Joseph in Egypt
1520	Birth of Moses
1440	The Exodus

BCE	Chapter 4: Lessons in the Desert
1440	A generation lives and dies in the wilderness

BCE	Chapter 5: Conquering Canaan
1400	Conquest of Canaan begins

BCE	Chapter 6: Period of the Judges
1400	Conquest of Canaan begins with fall of Jericho
1367	Israelites led by Othniel
1309	Israelites led by Ehud
1209	Israelites led by Deborah and Barak
1162	Israelites led by Gideon
1115	Ruth marries Boaz (grandfather of David)
1090	Israelites led by Samson
1050	Israelites led by Samuel

BCE	Chapter 7: Saul and David
1030	Saul becomes king, reigns 21 years

BCE	Chapter 8: David and His Sons
1009	David becomes king, reigns 40 years

BCE	Chapter 9: Solomon and Civil War
970	Solomon becomes king, reigns 40 years
966	Solomon builds Temple
930	Rehoboam becomes king, reigns Judah 17 years
930	Civil war divides nation into Israel (north) and Judah (south)
930	Jeroboam I becomes king of Israel, reigns 22 years
911	Asa becomes king of Judah, reigns 41 years
907	Baasha becomes king of Israel, reigns 23 years
885	Elijah's prophetic ministry begins
883	Omri becomes king of Israel, reigns 11 years

BCE	Chapter 10: Ahab and Jezebel
872	Ahab becomes king of Israel, reigns 21 years
870	Jehoshaphat becomes king of Judah, reigns 24 years
850	Joram becomes king of Israel, reigns 9 years
850	Elisha's prophetic ministry begins
846	Jehoram becomes king of Judah, reigns 5 years

BCE	Chapter 11: The Fall of Israel
841	Athaliah becomes queen of Judah, reigns 6 years
841	Jehu becomes king of Israel, reigns 23 years
840	Obadiah's prophetic ministry begins
835	Joel's prophetic ministry begins
835	Jehoash becomes king of Judah, reigns 34 years
818	Jehoahaz becomes king of Israel, reigns 16 years
802	Joash becomes king of Israel, reigns 15 years
801	Amaziah becomes king of Judah, reigns 18 years
787	Jeroboam II becomes king of Israel, reigns 39 years
783	Azariah (Uzziah) becomes king of Judah, reigns 51 years
780	Jonah's prophetic ministry begins
765	Hosea's prophetic ministry begins
760	Amos' prophetic ministry begins
750	Jotham reigns with Uzziah in Judah for 15 years
747	Menahem becomes king of Israel, reigns 9 years
740	Micah's prophetic ministry begins
740	Isaiah's prophetic ministry begins
737	Pekah becomes king of Israel, reigns 5 years
735	Ahaz becomes king of Judah, reigns 8 years
732	Hoshea becomes king of Israel, reigns 8 years
727	Hezekiah becomes king of Judah, reigns 30 years
722	Assyria destroys Israel

BCE	Chapter 12: Hezekiah, Manasseh, Josiah
727	Hezekiah becomes king of Judah, reigns 30 years
722	Assyria destroys Israel
697	Manasseh becomes king of Judah, reigns 55 years
640	Josiah becomes king of Judah, reigns 31 years
640	Nahum's prophetic ministry begins
640	Zephaniah's prophetic ministry begins
627	Jeremiah's prophetic ministry begins

BCE	Chapter 13: The Fall of Jerusalem
609	Jehoiakim becomes king of Judah, reigns 9 years
608	Habakkuk's prophetic ministry begins
605	Daniel's prophetic ministry begins
598	Jehoiachin becomes king of Judah, deported to Babylon
597	Zedekiah becomes king of Judah, reigns 11 years
593	Ezekiel's prophetic ministry begins
587	Babylonia destroys Jerusalem

BCE	Chapter 14: Exiled in Babylon
587	Final deportation of Jews to Babylon
538	Defeat of Babylon by Cyrus, King of Persia

BCE	Chapter 15: Restoration
538	Jews return to Jerusalem
520	Haggai's prophetic ministry begins
520	Zechariah's prophetic ministry begins
445	Nehemiah rebuilds Jerusalem's walls
444	Ezra reads the Torah scroll to Jerusalem Jews
430	Malachi's prophetic ministry begins

BCE	Epilogue
375	Syrian Aramaic increasingly replaces Hebrew
332	Alexander the Great conquers Palestine
323	Alexander dies, empire is divided among generals
312	Seleucus I rules Syrian portion of Greek empire
305	Ptolemy I rules Egyptian portion of Greek empire
275	Septuagint translation of Hebrew scriptures into Greek begins
167	Maccabean revolt against Antiochus IV
164	Rededication of the Temple
137	Jewish state established as Syria grants independence
63	Pompey conquers Jerusalem for Rome
37	Herod the Great named "King of the Jews" by Rome
19	Herod begins reconstruction of Temple
6	Birth of Jesus
4	Death of Herod

Glossary

Aaron – brother of Moses; priest of God; ancestor of all who would serve as priests (36-42, 45, 49-50, 59)

Abednego – name given to Azariah by Babylonian king (172)

Abel – the younger son of Adam and Eve, killed by his jealous brother Cain (16)

Abigail – widow of Nabal; wife of David (90)

Abner – military commander under King Saul (90-93)

Abraham – formerly called Abram; father of Isaac by wife Sarah and of Ishmael by Hagar (20-23)

Absalom – son of David; brother of Tamar; killed half-brother Amnon; usurped throne from David (100-104)

Achan – soldier who brought judgment on the Israelites for keeping plunder in violation of God's command (64)

Adam – in Hebrew "the man" who was first created and ancestor of all (14-16)

Adonibezek – Canaanite king who cut off thumbs of 70 kings and made them beg for food (69)

Adonijah – son of David; killed by Solomon for attempting to usurp the throne (106-109)

Ahab – seventh king of Israel (north); reigned 872-851 BCE; husband of Jezebel (120-134)

Ahaz – descendant of David; eleventh king of Judah; reigned 735-727 BCE (143-144)

Alexander the Great – extended the Greek Empire to Judea and much of the known world in 332 BCE (192)

Amasa – leader of Absalom's army; killed by Joab (104-105)

Amaziah – descendant of David; eighth king of Judah; reigned 801-783 BCE (138-139)

Ammonites – historical enemies of the Israelites; located on

East side of Jordan River (60, 73-74, 84, 185-186)

Amnon – son of David; raped his half-sister Tamar; killed by half-brother Absalom (100-101)

Amos – 8th century BCE prophet (139)

Antiochus III the Great – extended Seleucid rule within the Greek Empire (193)

Antiochus IV Epiphanes – decreed Judaism to be illegal within Judea; desecrated the Jerusalem Temple in 167 BCE (193-194)

Apocrypha – Hebrew scriptures from the intertestamental period included in some modern Bibles (194)

Aram – area including central Syria (69, 123-125, 132-133, 138, 144, 149, 192)

Ark of the Covenant – sacred box with Ten Commandments; kept in the Holy of Holies in the Tabernacle and Temple (48-58, 62-64, 79-80, 96-97, 111)

Artaxerxes – king of Persia (184-185)

Asa – descendant of David; third king of Judah; reigned 911-870 BCE (117)

Asher – son of Jacob/Israel and Leah's servant Zilpah (25-31)

Asherah – Canaanite goddess (120-121, 147, 152, 162)

Assyria – destroyed Samaria and deported residents of Israel (north) in 722 BCE (140-141, 143-158)

Athaliah – daughter of Ahab and Jezebel; usurped throne and reigned 841-835 BCE as Queen of Judah (125, 134, 137)

Azariah – descendant of David; also called Uzziah; ninth king of Judah; reigned 783-732 BCE (139)

Azariah – given name Abednego by Babylonian king in 6th century BCE; put in fiery furnace for refusal to bow down before idol (172)

Baal – Canaanite god (71, 120-128, 134-137, 152, 154, 161)

Baasha – descendant of Jeroboam; third king of Israel (north); reigned 907-884 BCE (117-118)

Babel – the site of the tower that would reach to heaven (18)

Babylon – city in modern Iraq; capital of Babylonian Empire; destination of Israelites deported during Exile (152-195)

Balaam – prophet who was called to curse the Israelites, but blessed them instead (60-61)

Barak – military commander of the Israelites who refused to lead his army unless Deborah accompanied him (70)

Baruch – scribe of prophet Jeremiah (158)

Bathsheba – widow of Uriah; taken by David; mother of Solomon (98-100, 106, 109)

BCE – "Before Christian Era" or "Before Common Era" used by scholars now in place of BC for "Before Christ"

Belshazzar – son of Nebuchadnezzar; last Babylonian king before overthrow by Medes and Persians (176)

Belteshazzar – name given to Daniel by Babylonian king (172)

Benjamin – son of Jacob/Israel and Rachel, who died in childbirth (26-31)

Bethel – town where Jacob/Israel settled after returning to Canaan with his wives and children (26, 115, 117, 135, 155)

Bilhah – servant of Rachel given to Jacob/Israel as a wife; mother of Dan and Naphtali (25-31)

Boaz – husband of Moabite woman, Ruth, and ancestor of David (78, 86)

Burnt Offerings – animals sacrificed within the Tabernacle or Temple (51-52)

Caleb – one of the spies sent into the Promised Land (59, 66)

Canaan – son of Ham; grandson of Noah; cursed by Noah for Ham's disrespect (17)

Canaan – the land promised to Abraham, Isaac and Jacob; home to descendants of Noah, Ham, and Canaan; home of Israelis and Palestinians in modern times (20)

Cain – the older son of Adam and Eve; killed Abel out of jealousy when God preferred Abel's offering to his own (16)

Covenant – agreement by which the Israelites promised to be faithful to the LORD God, who in turn promised to bless and protect the Israelites (45-56)

Cyrus – king of Persia; issued decree in 539 BCE that Jews could return to Jerusalem (175, 181, 183)

Dagon – Philistine god defeated in encounters with Ark of the Covenant and Samson (76, 79-81)

Damascus – Syrian city on northern border of Israel (117, 144)

Dan – son of Jacob and Rachel's servant Bilhah (25-31)

Dan – worship site established by Jeroboam (115, 117, 155)

Daniel – called Belteshazzar by Babylonian king; interpreter of dreams and visions; rescued from lions (172-177)

Darius the Mede – king of Medes who overthrew Babylon in 539 BCE (176)

David – son of Jesse; slayer of Goliath; second king of Israelites; composer of psalms (86-106)

Deborah – prophetess who led the Israelites as judge (70)

Delilah – Philistine woman who deceived Samson and robbed him of his strength by cutting off his hair (76)

Ebenezer – Israelite stone monument signifying "Thus far has the LORD helped us" (81)

Edomites – descendants of Esau; historic enemies of the Israelites; located in desert south of Dead Sea (60, 138)

Ehud – led the Israelites as a judge who conquered through deception (70)

Eli – Priest who raised Samuel (79)

Elijah – 9th century BCE prophet who confronted Ahab and Jezebel (120-128)

Elisha – 9th century BCE prophet whose mentor was Elijah (123, 127-134)

Esau – son of Isaac and Rebekah; brother of Jacob, to whom he lost his birthright and his father's blessing (23-26)

Essenes – separatist group dedicated to obeying the Torah; believed all others were Sons of Darkness (196)

Eve – in Hebrew "mother of all" who was created from Adam's rib to be his partner (15-16)

Ezekiel – prophet to exiles in Babylon (159-164, 178)

Ezra – scribe instrumental in renewal of the covenant through public reading of the Torah (181-187)

Gad – son of Jacob and Leah's servant Zilpah (25-31)

Gedaliah – governor of Judah installed by Babylonians after Jews were deported to Babylon (167)

Gibeonites – residents of Gibeon who tricked the Israelites into sparing them when Canaan was conquered (65, 97)

Gideon – led the Israelites as a judge; required much reassurance from God (71-73)

Goliath – giant and champion of Philistines slain by David (87)

Habakkuk – 7th century BCE prophet (156)

Hagar – servant of Sarah given to Abraham for the purpose of bearing a child; mother of Ishmael (21-22)

Haggai – 6th century BCE prophet instrumental in rebuilding the Temple (183)

Ham – son of Noah and father of Canaan; cursed by Noah for showing disrespect (17)

Hanani – 10th century BCE prophet (117)

Hananiah – given the name of Shadrach by Babylonian king; put in fiery furnace for failing to bow before idol (172)

Hannah – faithful woman whose son, Samuel, became a prophet, priest and judge (79)

Hanukkah – celebration of the rededication of the Temple in 164 BCE following its desecration by Antiochus (195)

Hasmonean Dynasty – priest/kings of Judea after Maccabean revolt until conquest by Rome in 63 BCE (194-195)

Hazael – assassinated king of Aram; usurped throne (133)

Hebron – city in which David (and later Absalom) was proclaimed king (92, 94, 102)

Herod the Great – Idumean appointed king of the Jews by Rome; undertook renovation of the Temple (195)

Hezekiah – descendant of David; twelfth king of Judah; reigned 727-697 BCE; promoted reforms (147-152)

Hoshea – nineteenth and last king of Israel (north); reigned 732-724 BCE (145)

Holy of Holies – innermost part of the sacred tent within the Tabernacle and Temple (48, 55, 111, 162, 194, 194)

Hosea – 8th century BCE prophet (139, 144)

Huldah – 7th century BCE prophetess (154)

Idumeans – inhabitants of Edom forcibly converted to Judaism during the Hasmonean Dynasty (195)

Isaac – son of Abraham and Sarah; father of Esau and Jacob by his wife Rebekah (22-24)

Isaachar – son of Jacob and Leah (25-31)

Isaiah – prophet whose ministry extended from 8th to 6th century BCE (139-153, 174-181)

Ishbosheth – son of Saul who sought to be king (93)

Ishmael – son of Abraham by Sarah's servant Hagar; ancestor of desert tribes (21-22)

Ishmael – assassinated Gedaliah in 5th century BCE (167)

Jacob – also called Israel; son of Isaac and Rebekah; brother of Esau; father of twelve sons and a daughter by two wives and their servants (23-31)

Jael – woman who killed Sisera through deception (70)

Japheth – son of Noah; with Shem, covered his father's nakedness and restored his dignity (17)

Jehoahaz – descendant of David; sixteenth king of Judah; reigned 609 BCE (158)

Jehoiachin – last descendant of David to reign in Jerusalem; eighteenth king of Judah; reigned 598-597 BCE; deported to Babylon (159, 164)

Jehoiada – 9th century BCE high priest who reigned on behalf of Joash until the king came of age (137-138)

Jehoiakim – descendant of David; seventeenth king of Judah; reigned 609-598 BCE (158)

Jehoshaphat – descendant of David; fourth king of Judah; reigned 870-846 BCE (125-128)

Jehu – tenth king of Israel (north); reigned 841-818 BCE (134-135)

Jephthah – prostitute's child who led the Israelites as a judge and sacrificed his daughter to fulfill a vow (73-74)

Jeremiah – 6th century BCE prophet during final years of Jerusalem before Babylonian exile (158-171, 181)

Jericho – the first city in the Promised Land to be conquered by the Israelites (63-64)

Jeroboam – commander of Solomon's workforce; first king of Israel (north); reigned 930-908 BCE; established worship centers at Dan and Bethel (113-118, 135)

Jeroboam II – thirteenth king of Israel (north); reigned 787-748 BCE (139)

Jerusalem – captured by David; established as capital city of David's kingdom; also called Zion (94)

Jesse – grandson of Ruth and Boaz; father of King David (86)

Jezebel – wife of Ahab (120-128, 134)

Joab – leader of David's army (93, 98, 101-105)

Joash – descendant of David; seventh king of Judah; reigned 835-801 BCE (137)

Jonah – 8th century BCE prophet sent to Nineveh (141)

Jonathan – son of King Saul and close friend of David (84-85, 88, 92, 97)

Joseph – favorite son of Jacob and Rachel; sold into slavery; rose to prominent position in Egypt (25-31)

Joshua – successor to Moses; led the Israelites into the Promised Land (59-67)

Josiah – descendant of David; 15th king of Judah; reigned 640-609 BCE; instituted reforms (153-158)

Jotham – descendant of David; tenth king of Judah; reigned 750-735 BCE (139)

Judah – fourth son of Jacob and Leah; offered to take Benjamin's place under Joseph's ruse (25-31)

Judas Maccabeus – led successful rebellion against Antiochus Epiphanes in 167 BCE (193-194)

Judge – political and military leader of the Israelites in the time before there were kings (69-71)

Laban – Jacob's uncle and father to Jacob's wives Rachel and Leah (25)

Leah – daughter of Laban; "unloved" wife of Jacob; mother of Reuben, Simeon, Levi, Judah, Isaachar and Zebulun (25-31)

Levi – third son of Jacob and Leah (25-31)

Levites – tribe of Levi set apart by God to serve priests and assist with Tabernacle and Temple (50, 59-61, 96, 188)

Lot – nephew of Abraham; resident of Sodom (20-23)

Malachi – final prophet of the Old Testament period (189)

Manasseh – descendant of David; thirteenth king of Judah; reigned 697-642 BCE; undid Hezekiah's reforms (152-153)

Medes and Persians – empire that overthrew Babylon and ruled from 539-332 BCE

Melchizedek – priest/king of Salem to whom Abraham gave a tithe of his plunder in gratitude for a blessing (21)

Meshach – name given to Mishael by Babylonian king (172)

Micah – 8th century BCE prophet (147)

Micaiah – 9th century BCE prophet sought by Jehoshaphat (125)

Michal – daughter of Saul; first wife of David (88, 90, 93, 96)

Midianites – country to which Moses fled (33); historic enemies of Israelites (35, 61, 70-73)

Miriam – sister of Moses (42)

Mishael – given the name Meshach by Babylonian king; put in fiery furnace for failure to bow before idol (172)

Moabites – historic enemies of Israel; lived east of Dead Sea in area now known as Jordan (60-61, 70, 78, 128-129)

Moses – deliverer of the Israelites from Egypt; leader chosen by God to communicate laws and enter into covenant (34-63)

Mt. Carmel – site of Elijah's battle with prophets of Baal and Asherah (121)

Mt. Moriah – site of Abraham's aborted sacrifice of Isaac (23)

Naaman – commander of Syrian army; healed of leprosy by Elisha (130)

Nabal – husband of Abigail; refused aid to David (88)

Naboth – owner of vineyard desired by Ahab; falsely accused and executed by Jezebel (124)

Nahum – 7th century BCE prophet (156)

Naomi – mother-in-law of Ruth (78)

Naphtali – son of Jacob and Rachel's servant Bilhah (25-31)

Nathan – 10th century BCE prophet; confronted David with adultery (97, 99-100, 106)

Nebuchadnezzar – 6th century BCE Babylonian king (159, 167, 172-173)

Nebuzaradan – 6th century BCE commander of Babylonian army (166)

Nehemiah – 5th century BCE governor of Judea under Persians; rebuilt the walls of Jerusalem (185-189)

Nimrod – a mighty warrior (18)

Nineveh – capital city of Assyrian Empire in modern Iraq (141)

Noah – the one good man in a world of evil who was chosen by God to build an ark and save his family and the animals (17)

Oded – 8th century BCE prophet (144)

Omri – sixth king of Israel (north); reigned 883-872 BCE; father of Ahab (118)

Othniel – the first to lead the Israelites as a judge (69)

Pekah – eighteenth king of Israel (north); reigned 737-732 BCE (142-144)

Pharisees – Jewish group dedicated to obeying the Torah and the oral traditions surrounding it (195)

Philistines – enemies of the Israelites in southern portion of Canaan (74-76, 79-80, 84-88, 91-92, 96, 127, 148)

Pompey – conquered Jerusalem in 63 BCE on behalf of Rome; desecrated the Temple (194)

Potiphar – captain of Pharaoh's guard who bought Joseph as a slave (27)

Priests – descendants of Aaron set apart to offer sacrifices within the Tabernacle and Temple (48-55, 59)

Ptolemy – ruled Egypt and surrounding areas on behalf of Greece after the death of Alexander the Great (192)

Rachel – daughter of Laban; beloved wife of Jacob; mother of Joseph and Benjamin (25-26)

Rahab – prostitute in Jericho who sheltered the Israelite spies and was spared when the city was destroyed (62-63)

Rebekah – wife of Abraham; mother of Esau and Jacob (23-24)

Rehoboam – son of Solomon; fourth and last king of united Israel; first king of Judah; reigned 930-913 BCE (114-117)

Reuben – oldest son of Leah and Jacob (25-31)

Rizpah – concubine of Saul; mother whose devotion to her slain sons led to their being buried with honor (97)

Ruth – Moabite daughter-in-law of Naomi who returned to Canaan with her and married Boaz (78)

Sadducees – group who accepted no scripture beyond the Torah; collaborated with Rome in ruling Judea (196)

Samaria – established by Omri as the capital city of Israel (north) (118, 120, 132, 144-145, 151, 182, 185)

Samaritans – inhabitants of Samaria and nearby areas; were converted to Judaism after being relocated by Assyrians

Samson – powerful fighter who defeated the Philistines, but carried out none of the other duties of a judge (74-76)

Samuel – 10th century BCE prophet and priest; the last judge of the Israelites before a monarchy was begun (79-86, 91-92)

Sarah – formerly called Sarai; wife of Abraham and mother of Isaac (20-22)

Saul – anointed by Samuel as the first king of the Israelites; reigned 1030-1009 BCE (83-93, 97, 102, 109)

Seleucus – ruled Syria and the surrounding area on behalf of Greece after the death of Alexander the Great (192)

Septuagint – Greek translation of Hebrew scriptures (192)

Shadrach – name given to Hananiah by Babylonian king (172)

Sheba – Benjaminite who led rebellion against David (105)

Shechem – first capital city of Israel's northern tribes (115)

Shem – son of Noah; covered his father's nakedness and restored his dignity; ancestor of Shemites, Semites, Hebrews, Israelites and Jews (17)

Simeon – second son of Leah and Jacob (25-31)

Sisera – Canaanite military leader killed by a woman (70)

Sodom – city in which Abraham's nephew Lot lived; destroyed by God for its wicked ways (20-23)

Solomon – son of David and Bathsheba; third king of Israelites; reigned 970-931 BCE; builder of the Temple; composer of proverbs (100, 106-114, 116)

Tabernacle – portable worship center containing Ark of the Covenant and altar for burnt sacrifices; built by Israelites in wilderness; used until Solomon's Temple was built (47-55)

Tamar – daughter of David; raped by half-brother Amnon (100)

Tammuz – Mesopotamian god (162)

Temple – center of worship in Jerusalem; location Ark of the Covenant; site of sacrifices; first Temple built by Solomon; second Temple by Haggai and Zechariah

Torah – laws and regulations of the covenant between the LORD God and the Israelites

Uriah – mighty warrior of David; husband of Bathsheba; put to death to hide David's adultery (98-99)

Uzzah – died after attempting to steady the cart holding Ark of the Covenant as it was being moved to Jerusalem (96)

Uzziah – descendant of David; also called Azariah; ninth king of Judah; reigned 783-732 BCE (139)

Zealots – dedicated to violent overthrow of Rome, much like happened during the Maccabean Revolt (196)

Zebulun – son of Jacob and Leah (25-31)

Zechariah – 5th century BCE prophet instrumental in rebuilding Temple (182)

Zedekiah – nineteenth and last king of Judah; reigned 597-586 BCE; blinded and killed by Babylonians (164-166, 170)

Zephaniah – 7th century BCE prophet (153-154)

Zilpah – servant of Leah given to Jacob as a wife; mother of Gad and Asher (25-31)

Zimri – fifth king of Israel (north); reigned 883 BCE (118)

Zion – another name for Jerusalem (170)